Novel Thinking Lesson Guide

Charlie and the Chocolate Factory

Other Novel Thinking Lesson Guides
Charlie and the Chocolate Factory
Charlotte's Web
Shiloh
In Their Own Words: Abraham Lincoln
George's Marvelous Medicine
Abraham Lincoln

Written By
Ryan P. Foley

Norman J. Larson

Graphic Design By
Danielle West

Anna Allshouse

Edited by
Stephanie Stevens

Patricia Gray

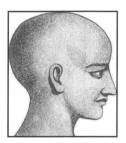
© 2008
THE CRITICAL THINKING CO.™
Phone: 800-458-4849 Fax: 831-393-3277
www.CriticalThinking.com
P.O. Box 1610 • Seaside • CA 93955-1610
ISBN 978-1-60144-175-1

Printed in the United States of America

ABOUT THE AUTHORS

Ryan P. Foley received his BA in elementary education from Loras College. He has been a fourth grade teacher since 2003. Mr. Foley has also taught special education students and has been a coach at summer camp.

Norman J. Larson received his BA in elementary education with a concentration in social studies from Clarke College. He has 15 post-graduate credit hours in the areas of literature and education. In 1999 he received National Board Certification as a Middle Childhood Generalist. He has been a teacher since 1994 and a fourth grade teacher since 1996.

The authors wrote these lesson guides after trying unsuccessfully to find existing quality materials for student use in order to teach novels effectively.

Table of Contents

Teaching Suggestions

Note: The page numbers referenced in this *Novel Thinking* guide correspond to the 2005 publication of *Charlie and the Chocolate Factory* (ISBN 0-14-240388-1). This guide can be used with any edition of the book, but the page references may be slightly different, depending on the edition.

The *Novel Thinking* books are student-oriented lesson guides, aimed at enhancing both reading comprehension skills and vocabulary. The intent is to provide structured, pragmatic, and easy-to-use supplemental classroom materials based on novels of interest to a particular grade level.

These lesson guides include the following language arts skills in the comprehension questions:

- Main Idea and Supporting Details
- Characters, Setting, and Plot
- Problem and Solution
- Cause and Effect
- Making Inferences and Predictions
- Drawing Conclusions
- Comparing and Contrasting
- Cause and Effect
- Sequencing

The table of contents includes the skills used in each exercise.

Vocabulary skills such as context clues, synonyms, and naming parts of speech are emphasized. Writing activities that use comparison/contrast and descriptive writing are also included.

Comprehension Exercises: Students are instructed to answer in complete sentences. Much of the study is directed to specific sentences in context and to author writing techniques. In cases where text is quoted, quotation marks must be used. This needs to be particularly emphasized to students when they copy something a character says or when quoting author text directly.

Scoring Methodology
Comprehension
Each question has a possible total of 10 points each.
- 5 points for content
- 5 points for grammar and punctuation

Students are awarded points based on the accuracy of their answers (content), and the format in which they provide the information (sentence structure). Setting a five-point range in each area allows the teacher to provide the student with an evaluation of student skills across a broader base.

All Other Sections
Each question is scored on content and points are indicated following each question.

Name: _____   Date: _____

Chapter 1: Here Comes Charlie
Chapter 2: Mr. Willy Wonka's Factory

A. Vocabulary: Write the underlined vocabulary word next to its definition below. Then name the part of speech (noun, verb, adverb, or adjective) for each word.

1. In the town itself, actually within sight of the house in which Charlie lived, there was an <u>**ENORMOUS**</u> CHOCOLATE FACTORY.

2. Like all extremely old people, Grandpa Joe was <u>*delicate*</u> and weak.

3. The factory had smoke <u>*belching*</u> from its chimneys and strange whizzing sounds coming from deep inside.

4. Charlie <u>*desperately*</u> wanted something more filling and satisfying than cabbage and cabbage soup for supper.

5. "Of course it's impossible!" cried Grandpa Joe. "It's completely <u>*absurd*</u>! But Mr. Willy Wonka has done it!"

6. Every one of Charlie's grandparents was as <u>*shriveled*</u> as prunes, and as bony as skeletons.

7. He has some really <u>*fantastic*</u> inventions up his sleeve, Mr. Willy Wonka has!

8. Walking to school in the mornings, Charlie could see the great <u>*slabs*</u> of chocolate piled up high in the shop windows.

9. Mr. Willy Wonka is the most amazing, the most fantastic, the most <u>*extraordinary*</u> chocolate maker the world has ever seen.

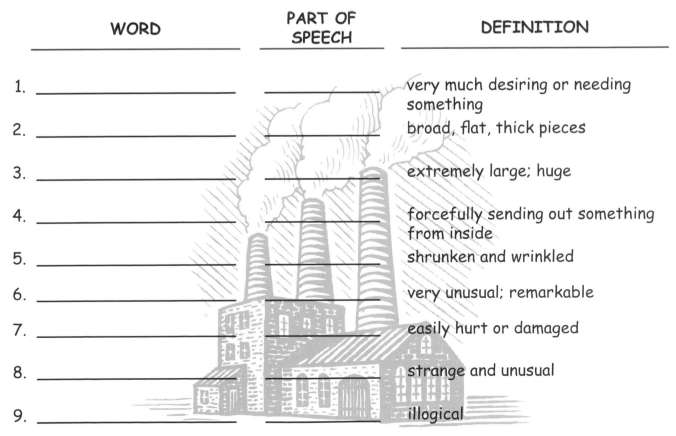

WORD	PART OF SPEECH	DEFINITION
1. _____	_____	very much desiring or needing something
2. _____	_____	broad, flat, thick pieces
3. _____	_____	extremely large; huge
4. _____	_____	forcefully sending out something from inside
5. _____	_____	shrunken and wrinkled
6. _____	_____	very unusual; remarkable
7. _____	_____	easily hurt or damaged
8. _____	_____	strange and unusual
9. _____	_____	illogical

B. Context Clues: Fill in the correct vocabulary word to complete each sentence. Use each word just once.

1. Most people think it is _____ to eat peas with a knife.

2. Bobby _____ wanted a new bicycle for his birthday.

3. For Mardi Gras, Jennifer wore a _____ costume with a lot of sequins and beads, along with a wild headdress.

4. The volcano was _____ flames, soot, and smoke.

5. The dinosaur had an _____ body but a small head.

6. The _____ flowers were lacking water and soon would die.

7. Grandma's hip bones were very _____, and we feared she'd fall and break her hip.

8. Jackie Robinson was not just a good baseball player but an _____ one.

9. For their patio, the Foleys poured several big _____ of concrete.

C. Characters: Match the correct letter of each character with the appropriate description.

A. Grandpa Joe

B. Grandma Josephine

C. Grandpa George

D. Grandma Georgina

E. Mr. Bucket

F. Mrs. Bucket

G. Willy Wonka

_____ 1. the mother of Mr. Bucket

_____ 2. the mother of Charlie Bucket

_____ 3. the father of Mrs. Bucket

_____ 4. the owner of an enormous chocolate factory

_____ 5. the father of Mr. Bucket

_____ 6. the father of Charlie Bucket

_____ 7. the mother of Mrs. Bucket

D. **Setting:** The setting is the "where" and the "when" of the story.

1. Give at least 3 details about the Bucket house. (page 4)

    a. _____

    b. _____

    c. _____

2. Give 2 facts about where the house was located. (pages 4, 7)

    a. _____

    b. _____

3. a. Does the story take place in the past, present, or future? b. Give at least 2
    details or observations from the book to support your answer. (page 5)

    a. _____

    b. _____

    _____

E. **Comprehension:** Answer the following questions in your own words using complete
    sentences. Use supporting details from the book where applicable.

1. Give at least 4 facts from the book that make you believe the Bucket family was
    poor. (page 4-6)

    _____

    _____

2. Describe Mr. Bucket's work. (page 5)

    _____

    _____

3. What did the Buckets eat at each meal during the day? (page 5)

    _____

    _____

    _____

4. Explain why everyone in the Bucket household looked forward to Sunday. (page 5)

   _____

   _____

5. What did Charlie long for more than anything else in the world? Give 4 details that prove that Charlie's "longing" was pure torture for him. (pages 6-7)

   Charlie's "longing": _____

   a. _____

   _____

   b. _____

   _____

   c. _____

   _____

   d. _____

   _____

6. Give at least 3 facts or details about Mr. Willy Wonka's chocolate factory. (page 7)

   a. _____

   _____

   b. _____

   _____

   c. _____

   _____

7. In the evening, when Charlie entered his grandparents' bedroom, what happened? Give at least 2 details. (page 8)

   a. _____

   b. _____

8. Describe Grandpa Joe. Give at least 3 details. (page 9-10)

   a. _____

   b. _____

   c. _____

9. Other than candy bars, describe the 7 other foods Mr. Willy Wonka invented. (pages 10-12)

   a. _____

   _____

   _____

   b. _____

   _____

   _____

   c. _____

   _____

   d. _____

   _____

   e. _____

   _____

   _____

   f. _____

   _____

   _____

   g. _____

   _____

Name: _____　　Date: _____

Chapter 3: Mr. Wonka and the Indian Prince
Chapter 4: The Secret Workers

A. Vocabulary Words: Use the definitions and the vocabulary words below to fill in the crossword puzzle.

colossal (page 12)	nibble (page 13)	dozing (page 13)	stammered (p. 14)
faint (page 18)	furnaces (page 16)	whirring (page 17)	spies (page 15)
deserted (page 16)	marvelous (page 16)	astonishing (page 16)	

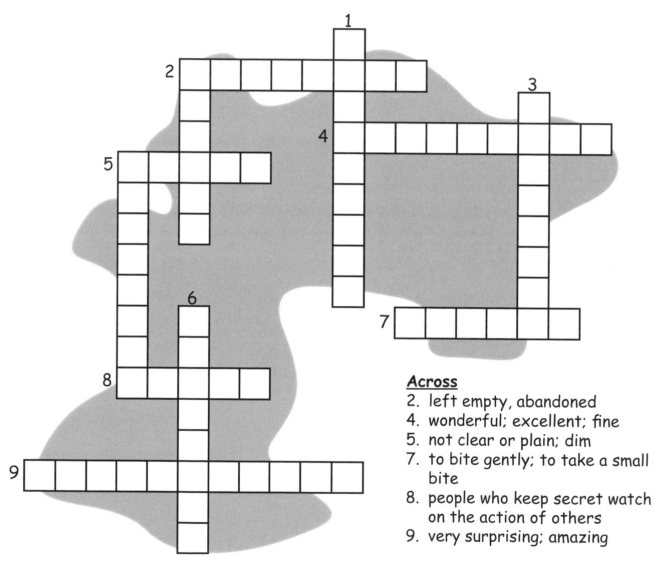

Across
2. left empty, abandoned
4. wonderful; excellent; fine
5. not clear or plain; dim
7. to bite gently; to take a small bite
8. people who keep secret watch on the action of others
9. very surprising; amazing

Down
1. repeated the same sound in an effort to speak; hesitated in speaking
2. sleeping lightly; being half asleep
3. of huge size; gigantic; vast
5. enclosed spaces to make a very hot fire in, to be used for heating places or melting items
6. moving so fast a buzzing sound is produced

B. Parts of Speech: Use the sentences and the dictionary to tell the part of speech (noun, verb, adverb, or adjective) of each vocabulary word. (You may also use the definitions from Part A to help you decide.)

1. Prince Pondicherry asked Mr. Wonka to come to India and build him a **_colossal_** palace entirely made out of chocolate.
2. The **_faint_** shadows that sometimes appear behind the windows are those of tiny people.
3. And suddenly, Wonka's giant chocolate factory became silent and **_deserted_**.
4. Prince Pondicherry was not going to **_nibble_** the staircase or lick the walls!
5. Someone's lit the **_furnaces_**! Mr. Wonka must be opening up again!
6. Mr. Wonka was so nice. And he made such **_marvelous_** things.
7. The crazy prince, who was **_dozing_** in the living room, woke up to find himself swimming in a lake of chocolate.
8. You can hear the machines! They're all **_whirring_** again!
9. Then something **_astonishing_** happened. Thin columns of smoke were seen coming out of the factory.
10. Mr. Wonka had to ask every single employee to leave and never come back because of **_spies_**.
11. "I...I really don't know, Grandpa," Charlie **_stammered_**.

Vocabulary Words

1. colossal _____
2. faint _____
3. deserted _____
4. nibble _____
5. furnaces _____
6. marvelous _____

7. dozing _____
8. whirring _____
9. astonishing _____
10. spies _____
11. stammered _____

C. Comprehension: Answer the following questions in your own words using complete sentences. Use supporting details from the book where applicable.

1. Describe what Mr. Wonka did for Prince Pondicherry. (page 12)

_____

_____

2. a. What happened to Prince Pondicherry's colossal palace? b. Describe what the prince was doing when this happened. c. What happened to the prince next? (page 13)

a. _____

_____

b. _____

_____

c. _____

_____

3. What did Charlie mean when he asked, "Or are you pulling my leg?" (page 13)

_____

_____

_____

4. According to Grandpa Joe, describe what was unique about the workers in Willy Wonka's factory. Give 2 details. (page 14)

a. _____

_____

b. _____

_____

5. a. Competing candy companies did a sneaky thing to make their products better. List the 4 things, in order, that they did. b. What effect did this have on Willy Wonka's Chocolate Factory? (pages 15-16)

a. _____

_____

_____

b. _____

_____

6. Although the gates of Mr. Wonka's factory were still closed, what led people to believe that it was working again? Give 5 details. (pages 16-18)

a. _____

_____

b. _____

_____

c. _____

_____

d. _____

_____

e. _____

_____

7. When people in town looked at the factory, what could they see? (page 17)

_____

_____

_____

_____

_____

8. Now, when Mr. Wonka invents some new candy, why are other candy makers unable to copy it? (page 18)

_____

_____

_____

_____

_____

9. What does Grandpa Joe say we know about the workers in the factory? (page 18)

_____

_____

_____

_____

10. a. Why has no one asked Mr. Wonka about whom he is using to do the work in his factory? b. What are the only 2 things that come out of the factory?   c. Describe how these things are handled. Give 3 details. (page 18)

a. _____

_____

_____

_____

b. _____

_____

_____

_____

c. _____

_____

_____

_____

11. Why was Charlie's father so excited when he came home from work? (pages 18-19)

_____

_____

_____

_____

Name: _____   Date: _____

Chapter 5: The Golden Tickets
Chapter 6: The First Two Finders

A. Vocabulary: Write the underlined vocabulary word next to its definition below. Then name the part of speech (noun, verb, adverb, or adjective) for each word.

1. Wouldn't it be something to open a bar of candy and see a Golden Ticket **_glistening_** inside!

2. The kids who are going to find the Golden Tickets are the ones who can **_afford_** to buy candy bars every day.

3. Great flabby folds of fat bulged out from every part of his body, and his face was like a **_monstrous_** ball of dough with two small greedy **_curranty_** eyes peering out upon the world.

4. Eating is his hobby, but still, that's better than being a **_hooligan_** and shooting off zip guns.

5. Fully grown women were tearing off the wrappers and **_peering_** eagerly underneath for a glint of golden paper.

6. "I don't think the girl's father played it quite fair, Grandpa, do you?" Charlie **_murmured_**.

7. He spoils her, and no good can ever come from **_spoiling_** a child like that.

WORD	PART OF SPEECH	DEFINITION
1. _____	_____	said in a soft, low, indistinct voice
2. _____	_____	huge; enormous
3. _____	_____	to have the money to buy something
4. _____	_____	a young person inclined to mischief
5. _____	_____	like a small, sour, red berry that grows on bushes and is used for jellies
6. _____	_____	shining as if it was wet
7. _____	_____	harming the character of a person by satisfying his or her every desire
8. _____	_____	looking closely to see clearly

B. Synonyms: A synonym is a word that means the same or nearly the same as another. Circle the word or phrase that is a synonym to each vocabulary word below.

1. **glistening**
   a. shining
   b. dull

2. **afford**
   a. a car
   b. has enough money

3. **monstrous**
   a. enormous
   b. mountain

4. **curranty**
   a. like a red berry
   b. new

5. **hooligan**
   a. a troublemaker
   b. a candy bar

6. **murmured**
   a. yelled
   b. spoke softly

7. **spoiling**
   a. playing
   b. indulging

8. **peering**
   a. eyeing
   b. sleeping

C. Comprehension: Answer the following questions in your own words using complete sentences. Use supporting details from the book where applicable.

1. Why would a child want one of the Golden Tickets? (pages 20-21)

   _____

   _____

2. Describe the Golden Tickets. Give 2 details. (page 20)

   a. _____

   _____

   b. _____

   _____

3. What 2 things might Mr. Wonka have to gain by putting out these special candy bars? (page 20)

   a. _____

   _____

b. _____

_____

4. Explain why Grandpa George thought Charlie had little hope of finding a Golden Ticket. Give 2 details. (page 21)

a. _____

_____

b. _____

_____

5. a. Who was the first child to find a Golden Ticket? b. What are 3 physical traits of the finder? (page 21)

a. _____

_____

_____

b. _____

_____

_____

_____

_____

_____

6. When Augustus found the ticket, how did the town celebrate? Give 2 details. (pages 21-22)

a. _____

_____

b. _____

7. a. Explain what Professor Foolbody invented. b. Describe what happened to his invention. (pages 23-24)

   a. _____

   _____

   b. _____

   _____

8. a. Who was the second lucky child to find a Golden Ticket? b. Give 3 details that help explain how her ticket was found. (page 24)

   a. _____

   _____

   b. _____

   _____

   _____

   _____

   _____

   _____

9. What are the similarities between the first winner and the second one? What are the differences?

   Similarities: _____

   _____

   _____

   _____

   Differences: _____

   _____

   _____

   _____

Name: _____   Date: _____

Chapter 7: Charlie's Birthday
Chapter 8: Two More Golden Tickets Found

A. Vocabulary: Write the underlined vocabulary word next to its definition below. Then name the part of speech (noun, verb, adverb, or adjective) for each word.

1. The old people propped themselves up on their pillows and stared with **_anxious_** eyes at the candy bar in Charlie's hand.

2. This **_particular_** candy bar had as much chance as any other of having a Golden Ticket.

3. All the grandparents and parents in the room were actually just as **_tense_** and excited as Charlie was.

4. **_Despicable_**! She'll come to a sticky end one day, chewing all that gum, you see if she doesn't.

5. There was great excitement in the Beauregarde household when the reporters arrived to **_interview_** Violet.

6. People were pushing and **_jostling_** and trying to get a bit closer to the famous girl.

7. It was not easy to hear all that she said because she was chewing so **_ferociously_** upon a piece of gum.

8. It's my most treasured **_possession_** now, this piece of gum is.

9. When the reporters arrived, young Mike Teavee seemed extremely **_annoyed_** by the whole business.

10. Mike was watching a film in which one bunch of **_gangsters_** was shooting up another bunch of gangsters.

WORD	PART OF SPEECH	DEFINITION
1. _____	_____	shoving, pushing, or crowding against; elbowing roughly
2. _____	_____	made somewhat angry, disturbed, or troubled
3. _____	_____	uneasy, nervous, or worried
4. _____	_____	one out of several
5. _____	_____	something a person owns
6. _____	_____	members of a gang of criminals
7. _____	_____	worried; eager; uneasy
8. _____	_____	to talk formally with someone to obtain information
9. _____	_____	having contempt for; feeling dislike for
10. _____	_____	fiercely; violently

B. Word Scramble: Use the clue to help you unscramble each vocabulary word.

_____ 1. EEIINRTVW A reporter wanted to do this with Miss Violet Beauregarde after she found a Golden Ticket.

_____ 2. CEFILOORSUY Violet chewed her gum in this way.

_____ 3. AEGGNRST Mike Teavee was watching a film about a bunch of these.

_____ 4. EENST Charlie's grandparents and parents felt this way when Charlie was opening the chocolate bar.

_____ 5. AINOSUX The grandparents' eyes were described this way when they saw the candy bar in Charlie's hands.

_____ 6. ADENNOY Mike Teavee was described this way when all the visitors and reporters arrived at his house.

_____ 7. AACILPRRTU The grandparents thought that **this** candy bar of Charlie's had as much chance as any other of having a Golden Ticket.

_____ 8. EINOOPSSSS A piece of gum was Violet's most treasured one of these.

_____ 9. ABCDEEILPS Grandma Georgina used this word to describe Violet.

_____ 10. GIJLNOST Reporters were pushing and doing this to get closer to the famous girl, the 3rd ticket holder.

C. Character: List at least 2 traits or facts about each of the following children. The pages listed are places where you might find some information, but you may use other parts of the book through Chapter 8. Write the page number where you found each trait or fact.

Character	Trait/Fact	Page	Trait/Fact	Page	Trait/Fact	Page
Augustus Gloop (pages 21-22)						
Veruca Salt (pages 24-26)						
Violet Beauregarde (pages 30-32)						
Mike Teavee (pages 32-34)						
Charlie Bucket (pages 4-7)						

D. Comprehension: Answer the following questions in your own words using complete sentences. Use supporting details from the book where applicable.

1. a. Describe Charlie's birthday present. b. Why was he nervous about opening it? (pages 26-27)

    a. _____

    _____

    b. _____

    _____

2. Give 3 details, in sequence, of how he opened the candy bar. (pages 27-28)

    _____

    _____

    _____

    _____

3. Describe how his parents and grandparents reacted when the candy bar was opened.   (page 28)

    _____

    _____

    _____

4. What did Charlie do after he opened the candy bar? Give 2 details. (page 29)

    _____

    _____

5. a. Who won the third Golden Ticket? b. Describe her reaction. (pages 30-31)

    a. _____

    _____

    b. _____

    _____

6. a. What record did the third ticket finder win? b. Before she went for the record, what trick did she like to play with her used gum? Explain why you think she did that. (pages 31-32)

a. _____

_____

b. _____

_____

_____

7. a. Who is the fourth ticket finder? b. How was his reaction different from the others? Give a detail to support your answer. (pages 32-33)

a. _____

_____

b. _____

_____

_____

8. What vocabulary word in a previous chapter would describe what kind of person he might be? Explain why.

_____

_____

_____

_____

_____

_____

_____

_____

_____

_____

Name: _____   Date: _____

Chapter 9: Grandpa Joe Takes a Gamble
Chapter 10: The Family Begins to Starve

A. Vocabulary: Write the underlined vocabulary word next to its definition below. Then name the part of speech (noun, verb, adverb, or adjective) for each word.

1. The old man gave Charlie a sly look, and then he started **_rummaging_** under his pillow with one hand.
2. It's my secret **_hoard_**, the others don't know I've got it.
3. The old man's fingers were **_trembling_** most terribly as they fumbled with the candy bar.
4. After the snow, there came a freezing **_gale_** that blew for days and days without stopping.
5. Nobody in the family gave a thought now to anything except the two **_vital_** problems of trying to keep warm and trying to get enough to eat.
6. As the cold weather went on and on, Charlie became **_ravenously_** and desperately hungry.
7. In these times of **_hardship_**, Charlie began to make little changes to save his strength.
8. Charlie would buy one **_luscious_** bar of candy and eat it all up right then and there.

	WORD	PART OF SPEECH	DEFINITION
1.	_____	_____	a very strong wind
2.	_____	_____	things saved and stored away secretly
3.	_____	_____	difficulty or suffering caused by a lack of something
4.	_____	_____	extremely pleasing to the sense of taste
5.	_____	_____	shaking because of fear, excitement, weakness, or cold
6.	_____	_____	searching randomly by moving things
7.	_____	_____	very important; absolutely necessary
8.	_____	_____	very hungrily; greedily

B. Synonym Chart: Write the vocabulary word that is a synonym to the words listed in the chart.

Synonyms	Vocabulary Word
1. essential; important	
2. shaking; quavering	
3. stash; treasure	
4. searching; ransacking	
5. tasty; delicious	
6. hungrily; greedily	
7. windstorm; tempest	
8. difficulty; misfortune	

C. Comprehension: Answer the following questions in your own words using complete sentences. Use supporting details from the book where applicable.

1. a. Describe, in sequence, what Grandpa Joe did the day after Charlie's birthday.
    b. What was Charlie's reaction? (page 35)

    a. _____

    _____

    _____

    b. _____

    _____

    _____

2. As they opened the candy bar together, why do you think Grandpa Joe tells Charlie that they do not have a hope? (page 36)

    _____

    _____

3.   a. As Grandpa Joe tore off the final piece of the candy bar wrapper, what did he
         and Charlie find underneath? b. Describe how they responded to the discovery.
         (page 36)

     a. _____

     _____

     b. _____

     _____

4.   Give at least 3 details about the cold weather and how it affected the Bucket
     family while inside their tiny house. (page 37)

Details About the Cold Weather	The Effect on the Bucket Family
_____	_____
_____	_____
_____	_____
_____	_____
_____	_____
_____	_____
_____	_____
_____	_____

5.   a. Explain what caused the Bucket family's meals to become even thinner.
         b. What did Mr. Bucket do to try to solve the problem? c. Was he successful?
         (page 38)

     a. _____

     _____

     b. _____

     _____

     c. _____

     _____

6. a. Explain why Grandpa Joe desperately felt that Charlie needed more food.
    b. What did he compare Charlie to? (pages 39-40)

    a. _____

    _____

    b. _____

    _____

7. What small changes did Charlie make to save his strength? (page 40)

    _____

    _____

    _____

    _____

    _____

8. a. What did Charlie find while walking back home one afternoon? b. What 3 observations did Charlie make after finding the item? c. What 2 things did he decide to do with this item? (pages 40-42)

    a. _____

    _____

    b. _____

    _____

    c. _____

    _____

9. Compare how Charlie behaves differently in this scene than anywhere in the book before.

    _____

    _____

    _____

    _____

Name: _____   Date: _____

Chapter 11: The Miracle
Chapter 12: What It Said on the Golden Ticket

A. Vocabulary: Write the underlined vocabulary word next to its definition below. Then name the part of speech (noun, verb, adverb, or adjective) for each word.

1. Charlie felt the joy of being able to **_cram_** large pieces of something sweet and solid into his mouth!

2. The sheer **_blissful_** joy of being able to fill one's mouth with rich solid food!

3. Don't tear it as you unwrap it! That thing's **_precious_**!

4. There was a **_peculiar_** floating sensation coming over him, as though he were floating up in the air like a balloon.

5. Grandpa leaned forward and took a close look. The others watched him, waiting for the **_verdict_**.

6. When it is time to leave, you will be **_escorted_** home by a procession of large trucks.

7. You will be able to keep yourself supplied with tasty **_morsels_** for the rest of your life.

8. I am preparing other surprises for all my beloved Golden Ticket holders— marvelous surprises that will **_entrance_**, delight, intrigue, **_astonish_**, and **_perplex_** you beyond measure.

9. Don't **_fluster_** poor Charlie. We must all try to keep very calm.

10. Swarms of newspapermen and photographers were pouring into the house. For several hours, there was complete **_pandemonium_** in the little house.

WORD	PART OF SPEECH	DEFINITION
1. _____	_____	accompanied; went along with a person or persons
2. _____	_____	puzzle; confuse; to trouble with doubt; bewilder
3. _____	_____	to force something into a space that is too small
4. _____	_____	to hold somebody's attention and produce a sense of wonder in the person
5. _____	_____	to make nervous and excited; confuse
6. _____	_____	strange; odd; unusual

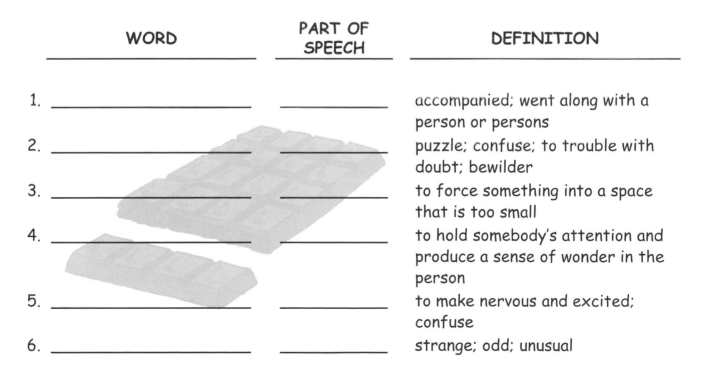

7. _____   _____   small portions of food

8. _____   _____   rare; not to be wasted

9. _____   _____   wild uproar or confusion

10. _____   _____   very happy and content

11. _____   _____   to surprise greatly; amaze

12. _____   _____   a judgment or decision

B. Synonyms in Context: Write the correct vocabulary word below for each underlined word or words.

cram (page 43)	precious (page 44)	blissful (page 43)	peculiar (page 45)
verdict (page 47)	escorted (page 50)	morsels (page 50)	perplex (page 50)
entrance (page 50)	astonish (page 50)	fluster (page 51)	pandemonium (page 53)

1. It was Grandpa Joe's final **decision** that the Golden Ticket was real.

    _____

2. On the back of the Golden Ticket it said that Mr. Willy Wonka was preparing surprises that would **awe**, **amaze**, and **puzzle** the guests.

    _____, _____, and _____

3. All the Buckets were excited about the Golden Ticket, but Mrs. Bucket was worried because she did not want anyone to **confuse** Charlie.

    _____

4. The shopkeeper told Charlie to be careful because the ticket was **of great value**.

    _____

5. For several hours, the reporters created **an uproar** in the Bucket house.

    _____

6. When Charlie found the Golden Ticket he got an **odd** floating sensation.

    _____

7. All the ticket holders would have plenty of tasty **bits of food** for the rest of their lives.

    _____

8. It made Charlie **very happy** to be able to **shove** large pieces of chocolate bar into his mouth.

    _____ and _____

9. After the tour of the factory, the ticket holders would be **accompanied** home by a procession of large trucks.

    _____

C. Comprehension: Answer the following questions in your own words using complete sentences. Use supporting details from the book where applicable.

1. Describe how Charlie ate the first candy bar he purchased. (page 43)

    _____

    _____

    _____

    _____

2. a. Describe what Charlie did when he picked up his second candy bar. b. How did the shopkeeper react? Give 3 details. (page 44)

    a. _____

    _____

    b. _____

    _____

3. Give at least 4 details about the attitude of the man behind the counter toward Charlie. (pages 43-46)

    _____

    _____

    _____

    _____

4. Several other customers made offers to Charlie in exchange for the Golden Ticket. What were 2 of the offers? (page 45)

_____

_____

5. What advice did the shopkeeper give to Charlie? Give 3 details. (page 46)

_____

_____

_____

6. How did Grandpa Joe react when he learned that Charlie had found the last Golden Ticket? Give at least 3 details. (pages 47-49)

_____

_____

_____

7. Describe the beauty of the Golden Ticket. Give 2 details. (page 49)

_____

_____

8. Summarize the message written on the Golden Ticket. (pages 50-51)

_____

_____

_____

_____

9. Who did the family decide will go with Charlie to the factory? Give at least 2 reasons the family selected this individual. (pages 51-53)

_____

_____

_____

Name: _____   Date: _____

Chapter 13: The Big Day Arrives
Chapter 14: Mr. Willy Wonka

A. Vocabulary: Write the underlined vocabulary word next to its definition below. Then name the part of speech (noun, verb, adverb, or adjective) for each word.

1. The crowd pushed and fought to get a **_glimpse_** of the famous children.
2. That's Mike Teavee! He's the television **_fiend_**.
3. Mr. Wonka wore a tail coat made of beautiful plum-colored **_velvet_**.
4. Covering his chin, there was a small neat pointed black beard—a **_goatee_**.
5. My dear boy, how good to see you! Delighted! **_Charmed_**!
6. Your grandfather? Delighted to meet you, sir! Overjoyed! **_Enraptured_**! **_Enchanted_**!
7. My workers are used to an extremely hot **_climate_**! They can't stand the cold!
8. Charlie Bucket found himself standing in a long **_corridor_** that stretched away in front of him.
9. Get a move on, please! We'll never get round today if you **_dawdle_** like this!

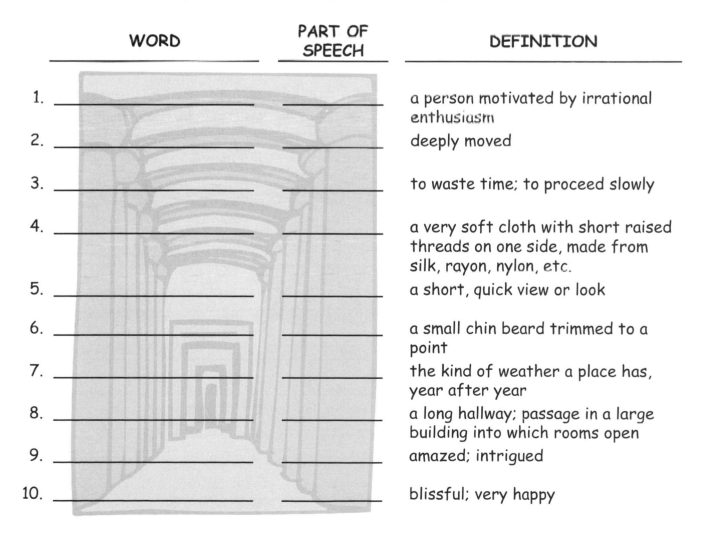

WORD	PART OF SPEECH	DEFINITION
1. _____	_____	a person motivated by irrational enthusiasm
2. _____	_____	deeply moved
3. _____	_____	to waste time; to proceed slowly
4. _____	_____	a very soft cloth with short raised threads on one side, made from silk, rayon, nylon, etc.
5. _____	_____	a short, quick view or look
6. _____	_____	a small chin beard trimmed to a point
7. _____	_____	the kind of weather a place has, year after year
8. _____	_____	a long hallway; passage in a large building into which rooms open
9. _____	_____	amazed; intrigued
10. _____	_____	blissful; very happy

B. Letter Placement: Use the word clue to identify the missing vocabulary word.

> glimpse, velvet, goatee, charmed, enraptured, fiend, climate, corridor, dawdle

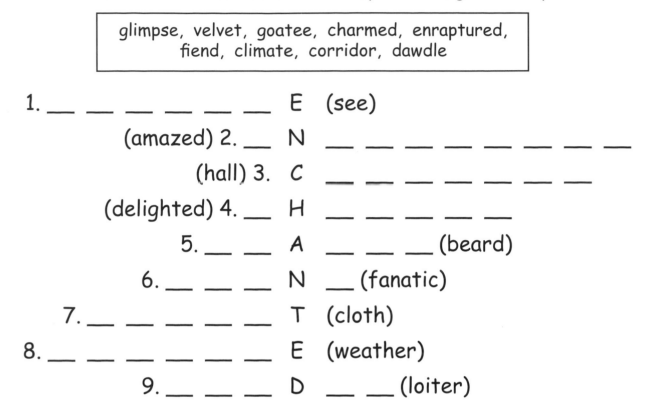

1. __ __ __ __ __ __ E (see)

(amazed) 2. __ N __ __ __ __ __ __ __ __

(hall) 3. C __ __ __ __ __ __ __ __

(delighted) 4. __ H __ __ __ __ __

5. __ __ A __ __ __ (beard)

6. __ __ __ N __ (fanatic)

7. __ __ __ __ __ T (cloth)

8. __ __ __ __ __ __ E (weather)

9. __ __ __ D __ __ (loiter)

C. Comprehension: Answer the following questions in your own words using complete sentences. Use supporting details from the book where applicable.

1. As the 5 children waited outside the factory, what made Charlie different from the rest? Give 2 details. (page 54)

_____

_____

_____

2. The crowd shouted things out as they identified the ticket holders. Write each name and describe what the crowd said about him/her. (pages 55-56)

_____

_____

_____

_____

_____

_____

_____

_____

_____

_____

3. Describe the appearance of Mr. Willy Wonka. Give at least 5 details. (page 57)

_____

_____

_____

_____

_____

4. How does Mr. Wonka greet his guests? (page 58)

_____

_____

_____

5. a. What reminder did Mr. Wonka give to the children as the tour is about to begin? b. Why?   (page 60)

    a. _____

    _____

    b. _____

    _____

6. Explain why Mr. Wonka kept the temperature in the factory so warm. (page 60)

_____

_____

_____

_____

7. Describe the large party of people following Mr. Wonka. (page 61)

_____

_____

_____

_____

_____

_____

_____

_____

_____

_____

8. a. Explain why all of the passages in the factory slope downwards. b. How does Mr. Wonka describe the most important rooms in the factory? (page 62)

a. _____

_____

_____

_____

b. _____

_____

_____

_____

Name: _____   Date: _____

Chapter 15: The Chocolate Room
Chapter 16: The Oompa-Loompas

A. Vocabulary: Use the definitions and the vocabulary words below to fill in the crossword puzzle.

insist (page 63)	valley (page 63)	froth (page 63)	alders (page 64)
flabbergasted (page 64)	delectable (page 66)	peals (page 68)	infested (page 69)
eucalyptus (page 69)	gorge (page 70)	smuggled (page 71)	mischievous (page 71)

Across
2. brought or taken secretly
7. full of pranks and teasing fun; naughty
9. to eat greedily until full; stuff with food
10. trees native to Australia with leaves that are the only food of koalas
11. a long lowland between hills or mountains
12. inhabited by quantities large enough to be harmful

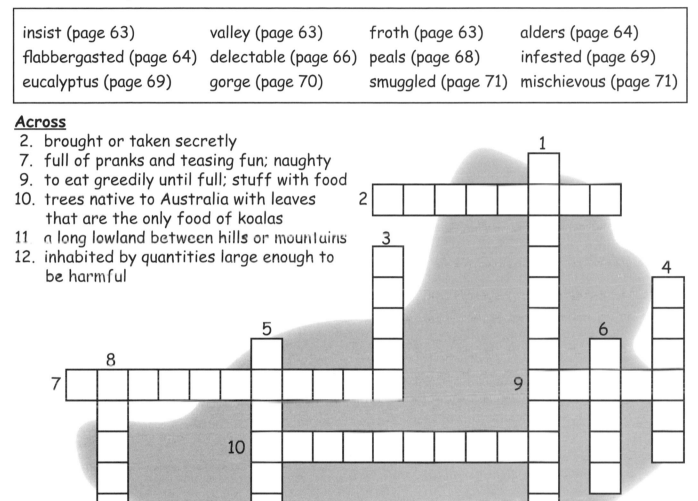

Down
1. speechless with surprise; greatly astonished
3. loud, long sounds
4. deciduous trees that grow in wet land
5. very pleasing to the sense of taste
6. a mass of very small bubbles formed in liquid; foam
8. to state, require, or demand something firmly

B. Parts of Speech: Use the sentences and the dictionary to tell the part of speech (noun, verb, adverb, or adjective) of each vocabulary word. (You may also use the definitions from Part A to help you decide.)

1. I _**insist**_ upon my rooms being beautiful! I can't abide ugliness in factories!
2. They were looking down upon a lovely _**valley**_. There were green meadows on either side of the valley.
3. There was a tremendous waterfall in which water went crashing down into a churning whirlpool of _**froth**_ and spray.
4. Graceful trees and bushes were growing along the riverbanks—weeping willows and _**alders**_.
5. The children and their parents were too _**flabbergasted**_ to speak. They were dumbfounded.
6. The grass is made of a new kind of soft, minty sugar. It's _**delectable**_!
7. The tiny men pointed towards the children and all five of them burst into _**peals**_ of laughter.
8. The thick jungles were _**infested**_ with the most dangerous beasts in the entire world.
9. The Oompa-Loompas spent their days climbing through trees looking for red beetles and _**eucalyptus**_ leaves.
10. You can have cacao beans for every meal! You can _**gorge**_ yourselves silly on them!
11. I shipped them over here. I _**smuggled**_ them over in large packing cases with holes in them.
12. I must warn you, though, that they are rather _**mischievous**_. They like jokes.

Vocabulary Words

1. insist _____
2. valley _____
3. froth _____
4. alders _____
5. flabbergasted _____
6. delectable _____
7. peals _____
8. infested _____
9. eucalyptus _____
10. gorge _____
11. smuggled _____
12. mischievous _____

C. Word Scramble: Use the question clue to help you unscramble each vocabulary word.

1. _____ ABCDEEELLT How did the grass taste in the factory?

2. _____ ADELRS What type of trees were growing along the chocolate river?

3. _____ ACELPSTUUY What leaves did the Oompa-Loompas use to help the green caterpillars taste better?

4. _____ IINSST The way Willy Wonka might strongly tell the Oompa-Loompas to keep the rooms beautiful.

5. _____ FHORT What formed at the bottom of the chocolate waterfall?

6. _____ CEHIIMOSSUV How did Willy Wonka describe the Oompa-Loompas?

7. _____ AELPS How was the laughter of the Oompa-Loompas described?

8. _____ EGGOR What would the Oompa-Loompas be able to do to themselves with cacao beans if they went to work for Willy Wonka?

9. _____ AELLVY What was the first thing the people saw when they entered the chocolate room?

10. _____ DEGGLMSU How did Willy Wonka get the Oompa-Loompas into the country?

11. _____ DEEFINST How did Willy Wonka describe the thick jungles and the number of dangerous beasts there?

12. _____ AABBDEEFGLRST How did the children and their parents feel when they saw the Chocolate Room?

D. **Comprehension:** Answer the following questions in your own words using complete sentences. Use supporting details from the book where applicable.

1. Give at least 4 details about the Chocolate Room. (pages 63-64)

   _____

   _____

   _____

   _____

   _____

2. What made Mr. Wonka's chocolate factory different from all others? (page 66)

   _____

   _____

   _____

3. As you've seen, the author uses many descriptive words to create pictures in our minds. List 8 adjectives you find on page 64, along with the nouns they describe (modify).

_____

_____

_____

_____

_____

_____

4. What caused Veruca Salt to suddenly scream and point frantically to the other side of the river? (page 67)

_____

_____

_____

_____

5. Describe the Oompa-Loompas. Give at least 3 details. (page 68)

_____

_____

_____

_____

6. a. What country did the tiny men come from? b. Give a description of this country. (page 69)

    a. _____

    _____

    b. _____

    _____

7.   a. What do the Oompa-Loompas like to eat? b. Why did they keep eating caterpillars? (page 69)

a.   _____

_____

b.   _____

_____

8.   How did Mr. Wonka convince the Oompa-Loompas to work in his factory? Give at least 2 details. (pages 70-71)

_____

_____

_____

_____

9.   What characteristics do the Oompa-Loompas show now that they work for Mr. Wonka. Give at least 4 details. (page 71)

_____

_____

_____

_____

10.   Two of the children were mentioned doing things that fit their characters as previously described by the author. Who were they, what did they do, and how did their parents respond? (pages 71-72)

_____

_____

_____

_____

Name: _____   Date: _____

Chapter 17: Augustus Gloop Goes up the Pipe
Chapter 18: Down the Chocolate River

A. Vocabulary: Write the underlined vocabulary word next to its definition below. Then name the part of speech (noun, verb, adverb, or adjective) for each word.

1. Mr. Wonka was hopping up and down and **_waggling_** his stick in the air.
2. Augustus Gloop could be clearly seen shooting up inside the pipe, head first, like a **_torpedo_**.
3. Where does that pipe go? Quick! Call the fire **_brigade_**!
4. Unthinkable! **_Inconceivable_**! Absurd! He could never be made into marshmallows!
5. Mr. Wonka thought no one would buy chocolate-covered Gloop. "They most certainly would!" cried Mr. Gloop **_indignantly_**.
6. If you leave him in the chocolate-mixing barrel too long, he's **_liable_** to get poured out into the fudge boiler.
7. Slowly the wheels go round and round, the **_cogs_** begin to grind and pound.
8. But this revolting boy, of course, was so **_unutterably_** **_vile_**, so greedy, foul, and **_infantile_**.
9. In the Oompa-Loompa song, they say Augustus Gloop was **_loathed_** by men.
10. The boat was a large open rowboat with a tall front and a tall back, like a **_Viking_** boat.
11. The parents were **_aghast_** when they thought Mr. Wonka had gone off his rocker.

WORD	PART OF SPEECH	DEFINITION
1. _____	_____	like an infant; babyish
2. _____	_____	hard to believe or imagine
3. _____	_____	likely; in danger of happening
4. _____	_____	a large metal tube that contains explosives and travels under water by its own power
5. _____	_____	struck with surprise or horror; filled with terror
6. _____	_____	unspeakably; not able to be expressed in words
7. _____	_____	angry at something unfair, wrong, or mean

8. _____   _____   moving quickly and repeatedly from side to side; wagging

9. _____   _____   a group of people organized for a specific purpose

10. _____   _____   felt intense dislike or disgust for someone or something

11. _____   _____   Scandinavian seafarers who raided the coasts of Europe from 700-900 A. D.

12. _____   _____   teeth on the rim of a gear wheel

13. _____   _____   very bad; evil; disgusting

B. **Context Clues:** Use a vocabulary word from the choice box to complete each sentence.

waggling (page 72)	torpedo (page 74)	brigade (page 75)	inconceivable (page 75)
indignantly (page 76)	liable (page 78)	cogs (page 79)	unutterably (page 79)
vile (page 79)	infantile (page 79)	loathed (page 80)	Viking (page 81)
aghast (page 85)			

1. The fire _____ was called to help control the forest fires.

2. When the townspeople saw the ogre, they were speechless because he was so

   _____ ugly.

3. The food was so _____, even the dog would not eat it.

4. The teenager threw a fit and began to cry, acting very _____.

5. Mark responded _____ when he was accused of being a liar.

6. The new nurse was _____ the first time she saw blood.

7. Amanda _____ having to stay home and baby-sit her annoying brother.

8. The idea of humans living on Neptune seems _____.

9. The chatterbox kept talking away. He didn't stop _____ his tongue for hours.

10. The long hours of work caused Nick to be run down and _____ to catch a cold.

11. The _____ boat sailed into the English harbor, prepared to take over the village.

12. When the wheel turned, the attached _____ pushed into grooves and put the machinery in motion.

13. The submarine fired its _____ at the approaching enemy ship.

C. **Comprehension:**   Answer the following questions in your own words using complete sentences. Use supporting details from the book where applicable.

1. There are cause-and-effect situations that develop throughout the disappearance of Augustus Gloop. Fill in the example below, then write out two more. (pages 73-74)

    Cause: <u>Augustus leaned too far over the riverbank.</u>_____

    Effect: _____

    _____

    Cause: _____

    Effect: _____

    _____

    Cause: _____

    Effect: _____

    _____

2. Explain the differences in attitudes between Mr. Wonka and Augustus' parents as Augustus went through his ordeal. (pages 74-78)

_____

_____

_____

_____

_____

_____

_____

3. What do you think the Oompa-Loompas meant when they were singing the following lines?

    "Augustus Gloop! Augustus Gloop!

    The great big greedy nincompoop!

    How long could we allow this beast

    To gorge and guzzle, feed and feast

    On everything he wanted to?

    Great Scott! It simply wouldn't do!"

Give at least 2 opinions/interpretations. (page 78)

a. _____

_____

_____

b. _____

_____

_____

4. Describe the boat that everyone traveled in to get to the next room. Give at least 3 details. (page 81)

_____

_____

_____

_____

_____

_____

5. a. What had Charlie Bucket seen so far that astonished him? Give a least 5 details. b. In your own words, tell why Charlie was so astonished. (page 83)

a. _____

_____

_____

b. _____

_____

6. a. Explain why Mr. Wonka gave only Charlie and Grandpa Joe a mug full of chocolate. b. Describe Charlie's reaction when he tasted the hot chocolate. c. What 3 things did Mr. Wonka say? (pages 83-84)

a. _____

_____

_____

b. _____

_____

_____

c. _____

_____

7. How would you feel about traveling with Mr. Wonka after hearing his song? (pages 84-85)

_____

_____

_____

_____

_____

_____

8. Some words on the three tunnel doors are a 'play on words.' a. What does 'play on words' mean? b. Give examples from those doors. (page 86)

a. _____

_____

_____

b. _____

_____

_____

_____

_____

_____

_____

_____

_____

Name: _____ Date: _____

Chapter 19: The Inventing Room—Everlasting Gobstoppers and Hair Toffee
Chapter 20: The Great Gum Machine

A. Vocabulary: Write the underlined vocabulary word next to its definition below. Then name the part of speech (noun, verb, adverb, or adjective) for each word.

1. Mr. Wonka exclaimed, "All my most secret new inventions are cooking and **_simmering_** in here."
2. "No touching, no **_meddling_**, and no tasting!"
3. The four children and their parents all **_scrambled_** after Willy Wonka.
4. "Over here I am inventing a completely new line in **_toffees_**!"
5. The saucepan was full of thick gooey purplish **_treacle_**, boiling and bubbling.
6. ...the glass tubes all curled downwards and came together in a bunch and hung **_suspended_** over an enormous round tub as big as a bath.
7. "It's a stick of the most amazing, fabulous and **_sensational_** gum in the world!"

WORD	PART OF SPEECH	DEFINITION
1. _____	_____	hard, brittle, or chewy candies made from molasses or brown sugar and butter
2. _____	_____	held in place by hanging
3. _____	_____	a blend of molasses, sugar, and corn syrup used as syrup
4. _____	_____	busying yourself with or in other people's things or affairs without being asked or needed
5. _____	_____	attracting a great deal of attention and interest; outstandingly good
6. _____	_____	moved in haste and a sense of urgency
7. _____	_____	to cook slowly in a liquid just below the boiling point

B. Odd One Out: Put a line through the word or phrase that is **NOT** related to the vocabulary word.

Vocabulary Word	Choice 1	Choice 2	Choice 3
1. meddling	intruding	being a busy body	trading
2. toffees	coffees	chewy candy	sweets
3. treacle	syrup	cereal	sweet goo
4. suspended	hung	flung	held
5. sensational	dimensional	attracting interest	awesome
6. scrambled	walked	moved quickly	hurried
7. simmering	almost boiling	thinking	cooking

C. Comprehension: Answer the following questions in your own words using complete sentences. Use supporting details from the book where applicable.

1. a. Which room in the factory did Mr. Wonka think is the most important? Explain why. b. Why did he keep everyone else out of this room? (pages 87-88)

    a. _____

    _____

    b. _____

    _____

2. Write at least 3 details about "the most important room." (page 88)

    _____

    _____

    _____

3. Do you believe Mr. Wonka loved this room most of all? Write at least 3 details from the book that justify your answer. (page 88)

    _____

    _____

    _____

4.   What marble-like invention had Mr. Wonka developed? Why is he inventing
     them? (pages 88-90)

     _____

     _____

     _____

5.   a. Describe what happened to the Oompa-Loompa who had eaten some Hair
     Toffee. b. What caused this to happen? c. What do you think this event says
     about Mr. Wonka? (pages 90-91)

     a. _____

     _____

     b. _____

     c. _____

     _____

6.   Give at least 3 descriptive details about the gigantic machine in "the most
     important room." (page 91)

     _____

     _____

     _____

     _____

     _____

     _____

7.   a. What object came out of the machine? b. Why did everyone think the object
     must be a mistake? (pages 93-94)

     a. _____

     _____

     b. _____

     _____

Name: _____   Date: _____

Chapter 21: Good-by Violet
Chapter 22: Along the Corridor

A. Vocabulary: Write the underlined vocabulary word next to its definition below. Then name the part of speech (noun, verb, adverb, or adjective) for each word.

1. "I want the magic gum!" Violet said ***obstinately***.
2. Charlie Bucket was staring at her absolutely ***spellbound***, watching her huge rubbery lips as they pressed and unpressed with the chewing.
3. Grandpa Joe stood beside Charlie, ***gaping*** at the girl.
4. There's almost nothing worse to see than some ***repulsive*** little bum who's always chewing gum.
5. She chewed while dancing at her club, she chewed in church and on the bus: it really was quite ***ludicrous***!
6. Just from chewing gum, Miss Bigelow was always dumb, and spent her life shut up in some disgusting ***sanatorium***.
7. The delicious smells came ***wafting*** through the keyholes.

WORD	PART OF SPEECH	DEFINITION
1. _____	_____	causing strong dislike or disgust
2. _____	_____	having your interest held completely by somebody or something; fascinated
3. _____	_____	floating easily and gently, as through air; drifting
4. _____	_____	amusingly absurd; very silly; ridiculous
5. _____	_____	a place for treatment of the sick or mentally ill
6. _____	_____	in a very determined way; stubbornly
7. _____	_____	staring in surprise with the mouth open

B. Which Word: Use a vocabulary word to answer each question.

obstinately (page 95)   spellbound (page 96)   gaping (page 96)   repulsive (page 99)   ludicrous (page 100)   sanatorium (page 102)   wafting (page 104)

1.   Which word is a synonym of *fascinated*? _____

2.   Which word tells about smelling something in the air? _____

3.   Which word might refer to a silly joke? _____   _____

4.   Which word describes how a stubborn mule might act? _____

5.   Which word describes a food you do not like? _____

6.   Which word is a place where people used to be placed to get well?

   _____

7.   Which word tells how you look at something that is ludicrous? _____

C. Comprehension: Answer the following questions in your own words using complete sentences. Use supporting details from the book where applicable.

1.   a. What did Mr. Wonka claim was his latest, greatest, most fascinating invention? b. Describe how Mr. Wonka thought this invention would change everything. Give at least 3 details. (page 94)

   a. _____

   _____

   _____

   _____

   b. _____

   _____

   _____

   _____

2. Mr. Wonka and the Beauregarde parents reacted very differently when Violet began chewing the gum. Write what those differences were. Give at least 4 details. (pages 95-96)

_____

_____

_____

_____

_____

3. In sequence, from beginning to end, describe what happened to Violet as she chewed the gum. Start by completing the first item. (pages 95-99)

Violet first tasted soup, then _____

_____

_____

_____

_____

1. a. Where did Mr. Wonka instruct the Oompa-Loompas to take Violet? b. Explain what they planned to do with her there. (page 99)

a. _____

_____

b. _____

_____

5. a. What happened to Miss Bigelow in the Oompa-Loompa's song? b. Why do the Oompa-Loompas want to save Miss Violet Beauregarde? Give 2 details. (page 102)

a. _____

_____

b. _____

_____

6. You've read how the first two children had things happen to them related to their bad habits. Use your imagination and write a short prediction about what might happen to each of the two children left. Remember to relate their fates to their particular bad behaviors.

_____

_____

_____

_____

_____

_____

_____

_____

_____

7. What are the names of the doors in the long pink corridor? Describe 5 items behind each door. (pages 104-106)

_____

_____

_____

_____

_____

_____

_____

_____

_____

_____

_____

_____

Name: _____   Date: _____

Chapter 23: Square Candies That Look Round
Chapter 24: Veruca in the Nut Room

A. Vocabulary: Write the underlined vocabulary word next to its definition below. Then name the part of speech (noun, verb, adverb, or adjective) for each word.

1. "There you are!" he cried **_triumphantly_**. "They're looking round! They are square candies that look round."
2. It makes the Oompa-Loompas **_tiddly_**. Listen! You can hear them in there now, whooping it up.
3. Twenty-five squirrels caught her right leg and **_anchored_** it to the ground.
4. "Why, to the furnace, of course," Mr. Wonka said calmly. "To the **_incinerator_**."
5. My daughter may be a bit of a **_frump_**, but that doesn't mean you can roast her to a crisp.
6. A fish head, for example, cut this morning from a **_halibut_**.
7. Who spoiled her, then? Who **_pandered_** to her every need? Who turned her into such a brat?
8. Who are the **_culprits_**? Who did that? You needn't look so far to find out who these sinners are.

WORD	PART OF SPEECH	DEFINITION
1. _____	_____	in a rejoicing way because of victory or success
2. _____	_____	a slang word that means drunk, as in having drunk too much alcohol; tipsy
3. _____	_____	a dull, unattractive girl or woman
4. _____	_____	provided anything someone asked for whether it was in their best interest or not
5. _____	_____	people charged with a crime
6. _____	_____	furnace or other device for burning trash and other things to ashes
7. _____	_____	any of several large flatfishes, used for food
8. _____	_____	set in place; attached firmly

B. Synonym: Circle the word or phrase that is related to each vocabulary word.

Vocabulary Word	Choice 1	Choice 2
1. tiddly	tipsy	tiny
2. pandered	roamed	spoiled
3. culprits	parents	lawbreakers
4. triumphantly	successfully	truthfully
5. incinerator	furnace	bonfire
6. frump	berry	dull woman
7. halibut	house	flatfish
8. anchored	fastened	climbed

C. Comprehension: Answer the following questions in your own words using complete sentences. Use supporting details from the book where applicable.

1. Everyone in the group except Charlie and Uncle Joe argued with Mr. Wonka about the Square Candies That Look Round. Which family was most argumentative and what things were said between them and Mr. Wonka? (page 107)

_____

_____

_____

_____

_____

_____

2. a. Explain what Mr. Wonka meant when he referred to square candies that look round. b. How did they resolve the argument? (pages 107-108)

a. _____

_____

_____

b. _____

_____

3.   Why didn't Mr. Wonka want anyone to go into the nut room? (page 109)

_____

_____

_____

4.   Give at least 3 details of what was going on in the Nut Room. (page 110)

_____

_____

_____

_____

5.   Why did Mr. Wonka insist on using squirrels to shell the walnuts? Give 2 reasons. (page 110)

_____

_____

_____

_____

6.   a. Describe how the squirrels could tell when a nut was bad. b. Explain what would happen when the squirrels find a bad nut. (page 110)

a.   _____

_____

b.   _____

_____

7.   a. What adjective do you think would appropriately describe Veruca? b. Give a detail to support your answer. (page 111)

a.   _____

b.   _____

_____

8. Write a brief summary of what happened to Veruca when she reached to grab the squirrel sitting nearest her. Give at least 3 details. (page 112)

_____

_____

_____

_____

_____

9. Why did the squirrels do what they did to Veruca? (page 112)

_____

_____

_____

10. a. Give 3 reasons why Mr. Wonka didn't seem particularly worried about the Salt family. b. How would you say Mr. Wonka and Charlie were alike in their reaction to this situation?   (pages 113-116)

a. _____

_____

_____

_____

b. _____

_____

_____

_____

11. Explain why the Oompa-Loompas suggested that it was appropriate for Mr. and Mrs. Salt to have suffered the same consequence as Veruca. (pages 117-118)

_____

_____

_____

Name: _____　Date: _____

Chapter 25: The Great Glass Elevator
Chapter 26: The Television-Chocolate Room

A. Vocabulary: Match the underlined vocabulary word with its definition. Then name the part of speech (noun, verb, adverb, or adjective) for each word.

1. One of the elevator buttons read, "Mint **_jujubes_** for the boy next door—they'll give him green teeth for a month."
2. "Take my hand, madam," said Mr. Wonka **_gallantly_**.
3. Then, as though the elevator had come to the top of the hill and gone over a **_precipice_**, it dropped like a stone.
4. They saw a great, **_craggy_** mountain made out of fudge, with Oompa-Loompas hacking hunks of fudge from it.
5. Charlie could hear the scream of the wind outside as the elevator **_hurtled_** forward.
6. There is dangerous stuff in here and you must not **_tamper_** with it.
7. The television screen **_flickered_** and then, lit up.

WORD	PART OF SPEECH	DEFINITION
1. _____	_____	a high, vertical, or very steep rock face
2. _____	_____	behaving politely and attentively, especially to women
3. _____	_____	shone with a wavering, unsteady light
4. _____	_____	to change other people's things without permission; meddle
5. _____	_____	steep and rocky; rough or uneven surface
6. _____	_____	moved or traveled at a high speed
7. _____	_____	fruit-flavored gumdrops

B. True or False: Tell whether each statement is true or false. Explain your answer using the vocabulary word in your explanation. Underline the vocabulary word.

1. <u>Jujubes</u> are sometimes sold at movie theaters. _____

_____

2. The bully acted <u>gallantly</u> when he shoved the girl into the swimming pool. _____

_____

3. It is safe to go sledding on a <u>precipice</u>. _____

_____

4. A rocket <u>hurtled</u> through the atmosphere to reach outer space.

_____

5. A mountain can be described as <u>craggy</u>. _____

_____

6. If you <u>tamper</u> with your neighbor's car, it will please him. _____

_____

7. It was easy to read the book while the lights <u>flickered</u>. _____

_____

C. Comprehension: Answer the following questions in your own words using complete sentences. Use supporting details from the book where applicable.

1. a. Name the people remaining with the tour. b. Explain what you think he meant when Mr. Wonka said, "They'll all come out in the wash!" (page 118)

   a. _____

   _____

   _____

   b. _____

   _____

   _____

2. Explain why Mr. Wonka suggested that the group take the elevator. (page 118)

_____

_____

3. Describe the elevator. Give at least 3 details. (page 119)

_____

_____

_____

_____

_____

4. a. What button did Mike Teavee select? b. What immediately happened to the elevator? Give at least 2 details. (pages 120-121)

a. _____

_____

b. _____

_____

_____

5. As the group traveled in the elevator, describe what strange and wonderful things they saw going on in some of the other rooms. Give at least 3 details. (pages 122-123)

_____

_____

_____

_____

_____

_____

_____

6.　Why were Mr. and Mrs. Teavee worried while riding on the elevator? (page 123)

_____

_____

_____

_____

7.　What did Mr. Wonka require the characters to wear inside The Television-Chocolate Room? Why? (page 124)

_____

_____

_____

_____

8.　Describe The Television-Chocolate Room. Give at least 5 details. (pages 124-125)

_____

_____

_____

_____

_____

9.　a. How were the Oompa-Loompas dressed in The Television-Chocolate Room? b. Describe how they were acting. Give at least 3 details. (page 125)

a.　_____

_____

b.　_____

_____

_____

_____

10. Describe the tremendous idea that Mr. Wonka had been struck by. Explain why he thought he could possibly do this. (page 127)

_____

_____

_____

_____

11. Why did Mr. Wonka insist that when a bar of chocolate is sent by television, it has to be big? (page 128)

_____

_____

_____

_____

12. a. Why were the Oompa-Loompas wearing space suits? b. What might happen if they weren't? (page 128)

a. _____

_____

b. _____

_____

13. What happened when Mr. Wonka told Charlie to reach out and grab the chocolate bar? (page 129)

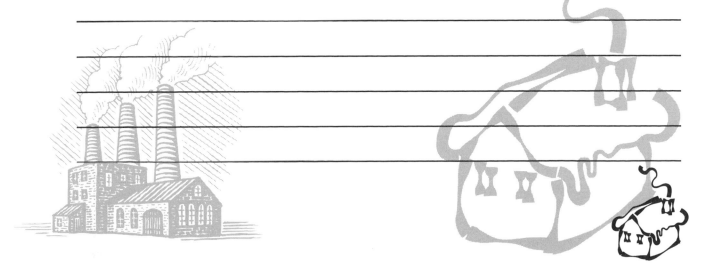

Chapter 27: Mike Teavee is Sent by Television
Chapter 28: Only Charlie Left

A. Vocabulary Words: Use the definitions and the vocabulary words below to fill in the crossword puzzle.

elastic (page 135)	loll (page 137)	nauseating (page 141)
arrangements (page 143)	craned (page 144)	splintering (page 145)

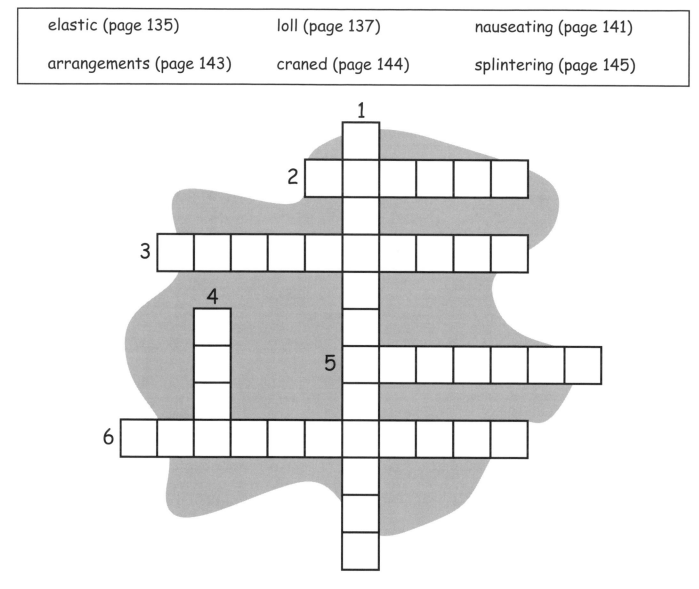

Across
2. stretched the neck in order to see better
3. causing to feel loathing, disgust, or sick to one's stomach
5. able to easily adjust to new or different conditions
6. splitting or breaking into thin, sharp pieces

Down
1. plans for how something will happen
4. lounge around

B. Synonym/Part of Speech: Write the underlined vocabulary word that is a synonym to each group of words. Then list the part of speech (noun, verb, adverb, or adjective) of the vocabulary word.

1. Small boys are extremely springy and **_elastic_**.
2. We've watched children gaping at the screen, they **_loll_** and lounge about, and stare until their eyes pop out.
3. Children will wonder what they'd ever seen in that **_nauseating_**, foul, unclean, repulsive television screen!
4. We have an enormous number of things to do! Just think of the **_arrangements_** that have to be made!
5. Charlie and Grandpa Joe both **_craned_** their necks to read what it said on the little label beside the button.
6. Then suddenly, CRASH!—and the most tremendous noise of **_splintering_** wood came from above their heads.

Group of Words	Synonym/Vocabulary Word	Part of Speech
1. stretched to see		
2. plan on how to do something		
3. to lean in a lazy manner		
4. sickening; disliking		
5. like a board split in many pieces		
6. adjustable; bendable		

C. Comprehension: Answer the following questions in your own words using complete sentences. Use supporting details from the book where applicable.

1. Mike Teavee asked Mr. Wonka if it is possible to send a real live person by television. a. Explain Mr. Wonka's response to Mike's question. b. Describe how Mike reacted after hearing Mr. Wonka's answer. (pages 130-131)

     a. _____

     _____

     b. _____

     _____

2. What happened to Mike Teavee once he reached the enormous camera? Give at least 5 details in sequence. (page 131)

_____

_____

_____

_____

_____

_____

_____

_____

3. What did Mr. Wonka say that scared Mr. and Mrs. Teavee? (page 132)

_____

_____

_____

_____

_____

4. What was Mr. and Mrs. Teavee's reaction to what happened to Mike? Give at least 2 details. (pages 132-133)

_____

_____

_____

_____

_____

_____

5. Once Mike appears on the screen, how is he physically different than he was before? Give 2 physical traits. (page 133)

_____

_____

_____

_____

6. Explain why Mike Teavee had a terrible tantrum. Give 2 details. (page 134)

_____

_____

_____

_____

7. a. Describe the plan Mr. Wonka had to help Mike grow. b. Why did he think it would work? (page 135)

a. _____

_____

b. _____

_____

8. In their song about Mike Teavee, what did the Oompa-Loompas suggest watching too much television did to children's minds? Give at least 5 details. (page 139)

_____

_____

_____

_____

9. a. What did the Oompa-Loompas tell parents they should do with their television sets? b. What did they recommend should take their place? c. Do you agree with these statements? Why or why not? (page 141)

   a. _____

   _____

   b. _____

   _____

   c. _____

   _____

10. a. Which children were still with the tour at this point? b. Explain what this means. (page 142)

   a. _____

   _____

   b. _____

   _____

11. a. What did Mr. Wonka suggest that Charlie, Grandpa Joe, and he do in order to speed things up? b. What was Charlie's reaction to this? (pages 143-144)

   a. _____

   _____

   b. _____

   _____

12. Describe what happened after Mr. Wonka pressed the button. Give at least 3 details. (page 144)

   _____

   _____

   _____

   _____

13. Explain why Mr. Wonka wanted the elevator to travel faster. (pages 144-145)

_____

_____

_____

_____

_____

_____

14. Describe what happened after the group hears a tremendous noise of splintering wood and broken tiles from directly above their heads. Give 3 details. (page 145)

_____

_____

_____

_____

_____

_____

15. What happened after Mr. Wonka pressed another button? Give at least 2 details. (page 145)

_____

_____

_____

_____

_____

_____

Name: _____   Date: _____

Chapter 29: The Other Children Go Home
Chapter 30: Charlie's Chocolate Factory

A. Vocabulary: Write the underlined vocabulary word next to its definition below. Then name the part of speech (noun, verb, adverb, or adjective) for each word.

1. He pressed a different button, and the elevator dropped lower, and soon it was **_hovering_** just above the entrance gates to the factory.
2. "You mustn't **_despair_**!" cried Mr. Wonka. "Nothing is impossible! You watch!"
3. Charlie climbed onto the bed and tried to calm the three old people who were still **_petrified_** with fear.
4. "There's one truckload for each of them, loaded to the **_brim_**."
5. Mr. Wonka **_cocked_** his head to one side.

	WORD	PART OF SPEECH	DEFINITION
1.	_____	_____	to lose hope
2.	_____	_____	staying in or near one place in the air
3.	_____	_____	paralyzed with fear, horror, or surprise
4.	_____	_____	to tilt or turn up or to one side a part of one's body
5.	_____	_____	the top edge of a container; full capacity

B. Word Play: Use a vocabulary word from the choice box to complete the phrase. The relationship between the first two words is the same as the relationship between the third and fourth words.

> Example: "hot is to cold as winter is to _____." Since the first two words are opposites, you need a word that is opposite of "winter" to complete the phrase.

hovering	despair	petrified	cocked	brim

1. big is to little as hope is to _____

2. happy is to glad as paralyzed is to _____

3. rabbit is to hare as suspended is to _____

4. room is to broom as rim is to _____

5. cold is to hot as straight is to _____

C. Comprehension: Answer the following questions in your own words using complete sentences. Use supporting details from the book where applicable.

1. What were the gigantic covered vans parked near the factory for? Give 2 details. (pages 147-148)

   _____

   _____

   _____

   _____

2. Describe each child after they "came out in the wash." (pages 148-149)

   _____

   _____

   _____

   _____

   _____

3. Why did Mr. Wonka think Mike Teavee is lucky? (page 150)

_____

_____

_____

4. a. What did Charlie think about Mr. Wonka's chocolate factory? b. Why was Mr.
    Wonka pleased to hear Charlie's response? (pages 150-151)

    a. _____

    _____

    b. _____

    _____

5. Explain why Mr. Wonka wanted to give his factory away. Give at least 3 details.
    (page 151)

    _____

    _____

    _____

    _____

6. Why did Mr. Wonka want to give his factory to a child? Give at least 3 details.
    (page 151)

    _____

    _____

    _____

    _____

7. Explain why Mr. Wonka decided to send out the Golden Tickets. (page 151)

    _____

    _____

    _____

8.   a. What caused Charlie to become gloomy? b. What solution does Mr. Wonka suggest to solve Charlie's problem? (page 152)

   a.   _____

   _____

   b.   _____

   _____

9.   How did Mr. Wonka suggest they get the bed out of the Buckets' home? (page 153)

   _____

   _____

   _____

   _____

10. How did Mr. Wonka, Grandpa Joe, and Charlie get everyone to ride back to the factory in the elevator? Give at least 2 details. (page 155)

   _____

   _____

   _____

   _____

11. Explain why Charlie laughed when Grandma Josephine asked if there will be anything to eat when they get to the factory. (page 155)

   _____

   _____

   _____

   _____

Name: _____   Date: _____

Descriptive Writing—Introduction

   Throughout *Charlie and the Chocolate Factory*, the five lucky children and their guardians are given an extensive tour of the factory by Mr. Wonka. During the tour, Mr. Wonka takes his guests into The Chocolate Room, The Inventing Room, The Nut Room, and The Television-Chocolate Room. While the characters are in each room, the author, Roald Dahl uses vivid imagery to help the reader paint a mental picture of each area. With the help of the characters, the reader is given insight into the unique sights, sounds, smells, textures, and tastes of each room.

   Your assignment is to write a descriptive paper on two other rooms in the factory. You may choose any **two** of the following:

1. STOREROOM NUMBER 54: ALL THE CREAMS – DAIRY CREAM, WHIPPED CREAM, VIOLET CREAM, COFFEE CREAM, PINEAPPLE CREAM, VANILLA CREAM, AND HAIR CREAM (page 86)
2. STOREROOM NUMBER 71: WHIPS – ALL SHAPES AND SIZES (page 86)
3. STOREROOM NUMBER 77: – ALL THE BEANS, CACAO BEANS, COFFEE BEANS, JELLY BEANS, AND HAS BEANS (page 86)
4. EATABLE MARHMALLOW PILLOWS (page 104)
5. LICKABLE WALLPAPER FOR NURSERIES (page 104-105)
6. HOT ICE CREAMS FOR COLD DAYS (page 105)
7. COWS THAT GIVE CHOCOLATE MILK (page 105)
8. FIZZY LIFTING DRINKS (pages 105-106)

   Once you have selected **two** different rooms, you need to create an illustration of what you think each room would look like. This will take a great deal of imagination and creativity. Remember to consider your senses when creating your illustrations. Once you have completed **two** illustrations, you are ready to begin the pre-writing piece of the writing project.

Name: _____   Date: _____

Descriptive Writing—Pre-Write
Descriptive Words and What They Describe

Directions: Use descriptive words and your senses to describe 2 rooms in the factory. List each sense used with your descriptive words (Sight - frothy chocolate or Touch - soft grass). You may use your illustrations as a reference.

1st Room: _____

_____

_____

_____

_____

_____

_____

_____

2nd Room: _____

_____

_____

_____

_____

_____

_____

_____

Name: _____   **Date:** _____

Descriptive Writing

Directions: Use a separate piece of paper to write 4 paragraphs using the instructions below. Do not use I, me, my, myself, our, we, you, your, or any other first or second person pronouns in your first three paragraphs.

Title: _____

Paragraph 1: An introduction stating what you will describe.
  a. Tell something interesting about the factory.
  b. Tell where it is located.
  c. 2 sentences

Paragraph 2: Describe one room in the factory.
  a. Topic sentence
  b. Use descriptive words and 2 or more senses to help the audience see, hear, touch, or smell this room.
  c. 4 sentences

Paragraph 3: Describe one room in the factory.
  a. Topic sentence
  b. Use descriptive words and 2 or more senses to help the audience see, hear, touch, or smell this room.
  c. 4 sentences

Paragraph 4: A conclusion summarizing what you have described.
  a. Closing paragraph
  b. Use at least 1 of the following conclusion strategies:
    • Summarize what you described.
    • Draw a conclusion about the factory from what you described.
    • Give your feelings/opinions about the factory.
  c. 2 sentences

Name: _____   Date: _____

Descriptive Writing—
REVISING Checklist

_____ Title

_____ Title is descriptive

Paragraph 1

_____ States what you are describing

_____ 2 sentences

_____ Is interesting

_____ Is on the topic

	__Topic Sentence__	__Indented__	__4 Sentences__	__Senses Used__
Paragraph 2 (1st Room)	_____	_____	_____	❑ Sight ❑ Hearing ❑ Smell ❑ Touch
Paragraph 3 (2nd Room)	_____	_____	_____	❑ Sight ❑ Hearing ❑ Smell ❑ Touch

Paragraph 4

_____ Closing paragraph: check at least one of the following conclusion strategies.

　　　_____ Summarizes what you described.

　　　_____ Draws a conclusion about the factory from what you described.

　　　_____ Gives your feelings/opinions about the factory.

_____ 2 sentences

Name: _____   Date: _____

Descriptive Writing—
Editing (CUPS) 2ⁿᵈ Draft

Directions: First, by yourself, make all the necessary changes in red on your second draft. <u>*Re-read each paragraph 4 times*</u>, checking for the following corrections:

      1. <u>*C*</u>*APITAL LETTERS*
      2. *WORD* <u>*U*</u>*SAGE*
      3. <u>*P*</u>*UNCTUATION*
      4. <u>*S*</u>*PELLING*

Next, have a partner give you suggestions and initial each part as you complete it together.

	Introduction Paragraph	Room 1	Room 2	Closing Paragraph
"C"apital Letters	You	You	You	You
	Partner	Partner	Partner	Partner
Word "U"sage	You	You	You	You
	Partner	Partner	Partner	Partner
"P"unctuation	You	You	You	You
	Partner	Partner	Partner	Partner
"S"pelling	You	You	You	You
	Partner	Partner	Partner	Partner

Name: _____   **Date:** _____

Descriptive Writing—
Grade Sheet

Use the checklist below to help score the writing project.

(Put in the grading scale used on the progress report card from the school.)

Grading Scale

_____ Plans and composes writing

_____ Revises writing   _____=_____

_____ Edits writing   _____=_____

_____ Communicates effectively using written language   _____=_____

_____ Applies spelling strategies to independent work   _____=_____

_____ Creates legible documents using cursive writing   _____=_____

_____ Title

_____ Title is descriptive

Paragraph 1

_____ States what you are describing   _____ Is interesting

_____ 2 sentences   _____ Is on the topic

	Topic Sentence	Indented	4 Sentences	Senses Used
Paragraph 2 (1st Room)				❑ Sight ❑ Hearing ❑ Smell ❑ Touch
	_____	_____	_____	
Paragraph 3 (2nd Room)				❑ Sight ❑ Hearing ❑ Smell ❑ Touch
	_____	_____	_____	
Paragraph 4				

Closing Paragraph:
Check at least 1 of the following conclusion strategies:

_____ Summarizes what you wrote.

_____ Draws a conclusion about the factory from what you described.

_____ Gives your feelings/opinions about the factory.

_____ 2 sentences

Name: _____   Date: _____

Comparing/Contrasting— Introduction

    After reading Roald Dahl's novel *Charlie and the Chocolate Factory*, you will have the opportunity to view the 2005 Warner Brothers' motion picture also entitled *Charlie and the Chocolate Factory*. The film was directed by Tim Burton and stars Johnny Depp as Mr. Willy Wonka.

    While watching the film, you will need a notebook and pencil to help take careful notes on any similarities or differences you notice between the novel and the movie. The notes you take will later assist you in writing a comparison/contrast paper on the novel and movie. Taking good notes will help you make a smooth transition to pre-writing and will enhance the overall quality of your writing project.

    Please use both the novel and your movie notes to help complete the pre-writing event sheet.

Name: _____ **Date:** _____

Charlie and the Chocolate Factory
Comparing and Contrasting Pre-Write
Novel/Movie Event List

Novel 	Movie 
Event	Event

Name: _____   Date: _____

Comparing/Contrasting Writing
1st Draft Directions

Directions: Use a separate piece of paper to write 4 paragraphs using the instructions below. Do not use I, me, my, myself, our, we, you, your, or any other first or second person pronouns in your first 3 paragraphs.

Title: _____

Paragraph 1: An introduction stating what you are comparing and contrasting.
   a. State the name of the novel and movie.
   b. Get your audience interested in reading your paper.
   c. 3 or more sentences

Paragraph 2: Comparing the similarities between the book and the movie.
   a. Topic sentence about who or what are alike.
   b. Give 3 or more details of events to support how they are alike.
   c. 4 or more sentences

Paragraph 3: Contrasting the differences between the book and the movie.
   a. Topic sentence about who or what are different.
   b. Give 3 or more details to support how they are different.
   c. 4 or more sentences

Paragraph 4: Close the paper by bringing your ideas together.
   a. Closing Paragraph: use at least 1 of the following conclusion strategies:
      • Summarize the main points.
      • Draw a conclusion about what you learned writing this paper.
      • State whether you preferred the book or the movie and why.
   b. 2 or more sentences

Name: _____   Date: _____

Comparing/Contrasting Writing
Examples of Topic Sentences

Comparing

1. The novel and movie have many similarities.

2. The novel and movie are alike in many ways.

3. The novel and movie are the same in many ways.

4. The novel and movie resemble each other in many ways.

5. The novel and movie have a few similarities.

Contrasting

1. The novel and movie have many differences.

2. The novel and movie are unlike each other.

3. The novel and movie are opposite in many ways.

4. The novel and movie do not have many differences.

5. The novel and movie have few differences.

Name: _____   Date: _____

Comparing/Contrasting Writing
Revising Checklist

_____ FOUR PARAGRAPHS (at least)

1ˢᵗ Paragraph: Introductory Paragraph
      _____3 sentences (at least)
      _____Introduce who or what you are going to compare and contrast.
      _____Get your audience interested in reading your paper.
      _____Give name of novel/movie.

2ⁿᵈ Paragraph: Comparing Paragraph
      _____4 sentences (at least)
      _____Topic sentence about who or what are alike.
      _____Tell how 3 events are the same.
      _____Give details of events from the novel/movie.

3ʳᵈ Paragraph: Contrasting Paragraph
      _____4 sentences (at least)
      _____Topic sentence about who or what are different.
      _____Tell how 3 events are different.
      _____Give details of events from the novel/movie.

4ᵗʰ Paragraph: Closing Paragraph
      _____Closing Paragraph: Check at least 1 of the following conclusion strategies:
         _____Summarize the main points.
         _____Draw a conclusion about what you learned writing this paper.
         _____State whether you preferred the book or the movie and why.
      _____2 sentences (at least)

Name: _____ Date: _____

Comparing/Contrasting Writing
Editing (CUPS) 2nd Draft

Directions: First, by yourself make all the necessary changes in red on your second draft. *Re-read each paragraph 4 times* checking for the following corrections:

1. *C*APITAL LETTERS
2. WORD *U*SAGE
3. *P*UNCTUATION
4. *S*PELLING.

Next, have a partner give you suggestions and initial each part as you complete it together.

	Introduction Paragraph	Comparing Paragraph	Contrasting Paragraph	Closing Paragraph
"C"apital Letters	You	You	You	You
	Partner	Partner	Partner	Partner
Word "U"sage	You	You	You	You
	Partner	Partner	Partner	Partner
"P"unctuation	You	You	You	You
	Partner	Partner	Partner	Partner
"S"pelling	You	You	You	You
	Partner	Partner	Partner	Partner

Name: _____ Date: _____

Compare and Contrast Writing Grade Sheet

(Put in the grading scale used
on the progress report
card from the school.)
<u>Grading Scale</u>

_____Plans and composes writing

_____Revises writing   _____=_____

_____Edits writing   _____=_____

_____Communicates effectively using written language   _____=_____

_____Applies spelling strategies to independent work   _____=_____

_____Creates legible documents using cursive writing   _____=_____

Use the checklist below to help score the process writing project

_____ Title
_____ Did not use the pronouns ***I, me. my, mine, myself, our, we, you, your*** or
         any other 1ST or 2ND person pronouns in the 1ST three paragraphs.
_____ Four paragraphs
1st Paragraph: Introductory Paragraph
         _____ 3 sentences (at least)
         _____ Introduce who or what you are going to compare and contrast.
         _____ Get your audience interested in reading your paper.
         _____ Give name of novel/movie.
2nd Paragraph: Comparing Paragraph
         _____ 4 sentences (at least)
         _____ Topic sentence about who or what are alike.
         _____ Supporting details: Tell how they are the same. (At least 3 events)
         _____ Give details of events from the novel/movie.
3rd Paragraph: Contrasting Paragraph
         _____ 4 sentences (at least)
         _____ Topic sentence about who or what are different.
         _____ Supporting details: Tell how they are different. (At least 3 events)
         _____ Give details of events from the novel/movie.
4th Paragraph: Closing Paragraph
         _____ 2 sentences (at least)
         _____ Bring ideas together, letting the readers know you are concluding your
                 paper.
         _____ At least 1 of the following conclusion strategies:
                 _____ Summarize the main points.
                 _____ Draw a conclusion (what was learned writing the paper—do you
                         prefer the novel or the movie?)
                 _____ Give your opinion on the novel/movie.

Name: _____   Date: _____

Extension Activity 1

What was your favorite part of the book? Why? Draw a picture of the event and write a description (caption) below it.

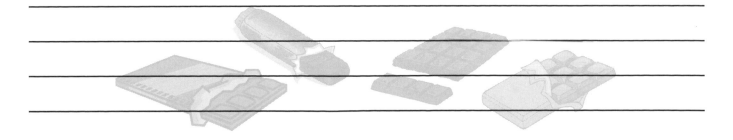

Extension Activitiy 2

Story Study Questions: Use a separate sheet of paper to answer these questions.

1.   Why do you think this story is enjoyed by so many readers?

2.   Do you think Charlie has any bad habits? Why or why not?

3.   What qualities does Charlie have that make him the hero of this story?

4.   Why does Mr. Wonka involve the parents in the trauma of their children's fate?

5.   How does the relationship between Grandpa Joe and Charlie change in the last part of the story? Explain your answer.

6.   What kind of person is Willie Wonka?

7.   How might modern readers criticize Mr. Wonka's treatment of the Oompa-Loompas?

8.   How do you think the Oompa-Loompas feel children should be raised?

9.   How would you describe the moral of the story?

10.   Do you think adults would enjoy this book? Do you think they would like the movie? Explain why or why not.

ANSWERS

Chapters 1 and 2

Page 1 A

Word	Part of Speech
1. desperately	adverb
2. slabs	noun
3. enormous	adjective
4. belching	verb
5. shriveled	adjective
6. extraordinary	adjective
7. delicate	adjective
8. fantastic	adjective
9. absurd	adjective

Page 2 B

1. absurd
2. desperately
3. fantastic
4. belching
5. enormous
6. shriveled
7. delicate
8. extraordinary
9. slabs

Page 2 C

1. B
2. F
3. C
4. G
5. A
6. E
7. D

Page 3 D

1. Students need 3 of these answers.
   - It was a small wooden house.
   - There were only two rooms.
   - There was only one bed.
   - It wasn't nearly large enough for so many people.
2. • The house is on the edge of a great town.
   - It is within sight of the chocolate factory.
3. a. The story takes place in the past.
   b. The drawings show people dressed in old-fashioned clothes.
   - We now have machines to do things like screw on toothpaste caps.

Pages 3-5 E

Sentences will vary.
1. • Their house was too small for so many people.
   - The house had only two rooms.
   - Life was uncomfortable for everyone.
   - There was only one bed.
   - The mother, father, and Charlie used mattresses on the floor for sleeping.
   - They were cold in the winter because they didn't have enough heat.
   - They were too poor to buy a better house or any more beds.
   - The father didn't make enough money to buy what they needed.
   - They didn't have the money to buy proper food: they ate just bread, margarine, boiled potatoes, cabbage, and cabbage soup.
   - They were hungry all day.
   - Charlie only received one small chocolate bar for his birthday.
2. Mr. Bucket worked in a toothpaste factory screwing little caps onto the tops of the tubes of toothpaste.
3. The Bucket family ate bread and margarine for breakfast, cabbage and potatoes for lunch, and cabbage soup for supper.
4. On Sunday, everyone was allowed a second helping of food.

5. Charlie longed for chocolate. Details: (in any order)

   a. When he walked to school, he saw great slabs of chocolate piled high in shop windows.

   b. Many times a day, he saw children taking creamy candy bars out of their pockets and munching them greedily.

   c. Charlie received only one candy bar a year, on his birthday.

   d. In sight of his house, there was an enormous chocolate factory—Willy Wonka's.

6. Students need 3 of these answers.

   • It had huge iron gates leading into it.

   • Smoke was belching from the chimneys.

   • Strange whizzing sounds came from deep inside it.

   • A high wall was surrounding it.

   • The air was scented with the heavy rich smell of chocolate.

7. Students need 2 of these answers.

   • His grandparents would sit up in bed.

   • Their wrinkled faces would light up with smiles.

   • They would start talking.

8. Students need 3 of these answers.

   • He was oldest of the 4 grandparents.

   • He was $96\frac{1}{2}$ years old.

   • He was delicate and weak.

   • He spoke very little throughout the day.

9. 7 other inventions of Willy Wonka (in any order)

   a. Chocolate ice cream that stays cold without being in an icebox.

   b. Lovely blue birds' eggs with black spots on them—when you put them in your mouth, they get gradually smaller until there is nothing except a little pink sugary baby bird sitting on the tip of your tongue.

   c. Marshmallows that taste of violets.

   d. Rich caramels that change color every ten seconds as you suck them.

   e. Little feathery sweets that melt away the moment you put them between you lips.

   f. Chewing gum that never loses its taste.

   g. Candy balloons that you can blow up to enormous sizes.

Chapters 3 and 4

Page 6 A

Down	Across
1. stammered	2. deserted
2. dozing	4. marvelous
3. colossal	5. faint
5. furnaces	7. nibble
6. whirring	8. spies
	9. astonishing

Page 7 B

1. adjective	7. verb
2. adjective	8. verb
3. adjective	9. adjective
4. verb	10. noun
5. noun	11. verb
6. adjective	

Pages 7-10 C

Sentences will vary.

1. Mr. Wonka went to India and built him a colossal palace made entirely out of chocolate.

2. a. The boiling sun caused the whole palace to melt.

   b. He was dozing in the living room.

   c. He woke up to find himself swimming around in a huge brown sticky lake of chocolate.

3. Charlie was asking if Grandpa Joe "was just joking or kidding around with him."

4. Students need 2 of these answers.
   - Nobody ever sees them go in.
   - Nobody ever sees them come out.
   - They are not ordinary people.

5. a. This is the sequence.
   - They sent in spies who pretended to be ordinary workers.
   - Each spy found out how a certain special thing was made.
   - The spies went back to their own factories with the recipes.
   - The factories begin making the same products as Willy Wonka did.

   b. Willy Wonka sent all the workers home and closed the chocolate factory.

6. Students need 5 of these answers.
   - Thin columns of white smoke came out of the chimneys.
   - People heard machines whirring.
   - People smelled melting chocolate.
   - People saw shadows moving around inside.
   - Packed and addressed boxes came out a trap door and were picked up by the Post Office.
   - Even better Wonka candies began to appear in stores for sale.

7. People standing on the street outside could see small dark shadows moving behind the frosted glass.

8. No spies can go into the factory to see how it is made.

9. Students need 1 of these answers.
   - They are very small.
   - The faint shadows that appear behind the windows are those of tiny people.

10. a. No one sees him any more. He never comes out. (in any order)

b. Only chocolates and candies come out of the factory.

c. They come out through a special trap door, all packed and addressed, and they are picked up every day by the Post Office.

11. The headline on the newspaper he carried read "Wonka Factory to be Opened at Last to Lucky Few."

Chapters 5 and 6

Page 11 A

Word	Part of Speech
1. murmured	verb
2. monstrous	adjective
3. afford	verb
4. hooligan	noun
5. curranty	adjective
6. glistening	verb
7. spoiling	verb
8. peering	verb

Page 12 B

1. a	5. a
2. b	6. b
3. a	7. b
4. a	8. a

Pages 12-14 C
Sentences will vary.

1. Students need 1 of these answers.
   - He or she would visit the factory.
   - Each winner would be supplied with a lifetime of free chocolate and candies.

2. a. They are printed on golden paper.
   b. They have been hidden underneath the ordinary wrapping paper of 5 ordinary candy bars.

3. Students need 2 of these answers.
   - It would receive a lot of attention and advertise his product.

- He'd sell a lot of chocolate bars.
- He'd make more money.

4. (in any order)
   a. He says the kids who are going to find the Golden Tickets are the ones who can afford to buy candy bars everyday.
   b. Charlie only gets a candy bar once a year for his birthday.

5. a. Augustus Gloop was the first winner.
   b. Students need 3 of these answers.
   - He was enormously fat.
   - He had great flabby folds of fat bulging out of every part of his body.
   - His face was like a monstrous ball of dough.
   - He had two small greedy currant eyes peering out upon the world.

6. Students need 2 of these answers.
   - Flags were flying from all the windows.
   - Children had been given a holiday from school.
   - A parade was being organized.

7. a. He invented a machine that could tell if a candy bar had a Golden Ticket in it.
   b. The crowd smashed the machine.

8. a. Veruca Salt was the next winner.
   b. (in any order)
   - Her father went into town and bought hundreds of thousands of candy bars.
   - He had them loaded onto trucks and sent them directly to his peanut factory.
   - He had the workers in his factory shell the wrappers off the candy bars instead of shelling peanuts.

9. Similarities:
   - Both have parents who give them whatever they want.

- Both are able to afford or eat lots of chocolate bars.
- Both had their pictures in the paper when they won.

Differences:
- One was a boy and the other was a girl.
- Veruca's father was rich.
- Veruca's father bought hundreds of thousands of bars and paid his employees to open the wrappers.
- Augustus ate all the chocolate bars he could have.
- Veruca had tantrums when she didn't get what she wanted.

Chapters 7 and 8

Page 15 A

Word	Part of Speech
1. jostling	verb
2. annoyed	adjective
3. tense	adjective
4. particular	adjective
5. possession	noun
6. gangster	noun
7. anxious	adjective
8. interview	verb
9. despicable	adjective
10. ferociously	adverb

Page 16 B

1. interview
2. ferociously
3. gangster
4. tense
5. anxious
6. annoyed
7. particular
8. possession
9. despicable
10. jostling

<u>**Page 16 C**</u>

Answers will vary - students need at least 2 answers. Possible answers are listed below.

Augustus Gloop
Fact/(Page #)
- 9 year old boy (21)
- Curranty eyes (21)
- Enormously fat (21)
- Eating is his hobby (22)
- Face is a monstrous ball of dough (21)

Veruca Salt
Fact/(Page #)
- Small girl (24)
- Kicks and yells in a disturbing way (24)
- Lives with rich parents (24)
- Spoiled (26)

Violet Bauregarde
Fact/(Page #)
- Talks fast and loudly (31)
- Gum is a treasured possession (31)
- Gum chewer (31)
- Disrespectful to mother (31)
- Sticks gum on different objects (31-32)

Mike Teavee
Fact/(Page #)
- Annoyed by reporters (32)
- Wears 18 toy pistols (33)
- 9 year-old boy (33)
- Rude (33-34)
- Constantly watching TV (33)

Charlie Bucket
Fact/(Page #)
- Lives in 2 room house (4)
- Lives with parents and grandparents (4)
- Sleeps on mattress on floor (5)

- Longs for chocolate (6)
- Gets a chocolate bar for his birthday (6)
- Wants to see inside of chocolate factory (7)

<u>**Page 17-18 D**</u>
Sentences will vary.
1. • Charlie's present was a Wonka Whipple—Scrumptious Fudgemallow Delight candy bar.
   • He was hoping there was a Golden Ticket inside the wrapper.
2. • He ran his fingers back and forth along the length of the bar.
   • He slowly began to tear open one small corner of the wrapping paper.
   • He suddenly tore the wrapper open down the middle.
3. They all watched him to see what his reaction was.
4. • He offered everyone a bite of his candy bar.
   • Then he went to school.
5. a. Violet Beauregarde was the third winner.
   b. She waved the ticket and tried to talk, but she was chewing her gum too hard to be easily understood.
6. a. The record for chewing the same piece of gum for the longest time.
   b. Explanations may vary. She would stick it on a button on the elevator. It would stick on people's fingers. She thought it was funny.
7. a. Mike Teavee was the fourth winner.
   b. He seemed to be extremely annoyed about the whole thing.
   • He shouted at the reporters to be quiet and not to interrupt his TV show.

8. Hooligan. Because he'd be doing things that would get him in trouble a lot.

Chapters 9 and 10

Page 19 A

Word	Part of Speech
1. gale	noun
2. hoard	noun
3. hardship	noun
4. luscious	adjective
5. trembling	verb
6. rummaging	verb
7. vital	adjective
8. ravenously	adverb

Page 20 B

1. vital
2. trembling
3. hoard
4. rummaging
5. luscious
6. ravenously
7. gale
8. hardship

Pages 20-22 C
Sentences will vary.
1. a. He beckoned Charlie to come closer.
   - He started rummaging under his pillow.
   - He pulled out a leather purse.
   - He opened the purse.
   - He tipped it upside down and a silver ten-cent piece fell out.
   b. (in order)
   - He asked Grandpa Joe if he was sure he wanted to spend his money on a candy bar.
   - He took the money.
   - He ran to the nearest store.
   - He bought the first Wonka candy bar he saw.
   - He brought it straight back to Grandpa Joe.
   - They opened it together.

2. Students need 1 of these answers.
   - Grandpa Joe didn't want to get the hopes of Charlie and himself up too much.
   - To lessen the inevitable disappointment.
3. - They found a candy bar, nothing else.
   - They saw the funny side of the whole thing, and they burst into peals of laughter.
4. Details of Cold Weather
   Students need 3 of these answers.
   - Huge flakes drifted slowly down.
   - There was an icy sky that was the color of steel.
   - Snow lay four feet deep around the tiny house.
   - A freezing gale blew for days and days.
   - Little jets of freezing air came rushing in through the sides of the windows and under the doors.
   The Effect on the Bucket Family
   - The old ones lay silent and huddled in their bed.
   - The excitement over the Golden Ticket was forgotten.
   - Nobody in the family gave a thought now to anything except the 2 vital problems of trying to keep warm and trying to get enough to eat.
5. a. Mr. Bucket lost his job—the toothpaste factory where he worked went bust and had to close down.
   b. He earned a few pennies by shoveling snow in the streets.
   c. No, it wasn't enough to buy even a quarter of the food that 7 people needed.
6. a. Because he's a growing boy.
   b. A skeleton.
7. - In the mornings, he left the house 10 minutes earlier so that

he could walk slowly to school, without having to run
- He sat quietly in the classroom during recess, resting himself, while the others rushed outdoors and threw snowballs and wrestled in the snow.

8. a. He found a dollar bill.
   b. Students need 3 of these answers.
   - The dollar meant food.
   - He saw a newspaper and stationery store close by.
   - He knew it was the kind of store that sold candy.
   - The store would have chocolate.
   c. (in any order)
   - He would buy one candy bar and eat it all up.
   - He would take the rest of the money home to his mother.

9. - He thinks only of himself in buying the two chocolate bars.
   - In comparison, up until now, he's been kind and considerate, accepting his poverty, his inadequate housing, and his hunger and never complaining.

Chapters 11 and 12

Page 23 A

Word	Part of Speech
1. escorted	verb
2. perplex	verb
3. cram	verb
4. entrance	verb
5. fluster	verb
6. peculiar	adjective
7. morsels	noun
8. precious	adjective
9. pandemonium	noun

Word	Part of Speech
10. blissful	adjective
11. astonish	verb
12. verdict	noun

Page 24 B

1. verdict
2. entrance, astonish, perplex
3. fluster
4. precious
5. pandemonium
6. peculiar
7. morsels
8. blissful, cram
9. escorted

Pages 25-26 C

Sentences will vary.
1. Charlie grabbed the bar, ripped off the wrapper, and took a huge bite.
2. Students need 4 of these answers.
   - He said Charlie looked like he really wanted the candy bar.
   - He was afraid Charlie would get a stomach ache.
   - He jumped up and down screaming when he saw the Golden Ticket.
   - He told Charlie to be careful and not tear it.
   - He finally took Charlie by the arm and told people to leave him alone.
   - He told Charlie to take the ticket and run home with it.
   - He told Charlie he, "had a feeling you needed a break like this." Then he said, "I'm awfully glad you got it."
3. a. Charlie tore off the wrapper and saw gold.
   b. (in any order)
   - He was excited.
   - He was yelling.
   - He looked like he might be going to have a fit.

4. (in any order)
   - A man offered him $50 and a bicycle as well.
   - A woman offered to give him $500 for the ticket.

5. (in any order)
   - Don't let anybody have it.
   - Take it straight home before you lose it.
   - Run all the way and don't stop until you get there.

6. Students need 3 of these answers.
   - He was overjoyed.
   - He had a slow and marvelous grin.
   - He was happy.
   - He looked straight at Charlie.
   - The color was rushing to his cheeks.
   - His eyes were wide open shining with joy.
   - A little spark of wild excitement was slowly dancing in the center of each eye.
   - An explosion seemed to take place inside him.
   - He yelled, "Yippeee!"
   - He jumped on to the floor and started doing a dance of victory in his pajamas.

7. (in any order)
   - It seemed to be made from a sheet of pure gold hammered out almost to the thinness of paper.
   - On one side of it, printed by some clever method in jet black letters, was the invitation itself—from Mr. Wonka.

8. Summary may include the following.
   - On February 1st you must come to the factory at 10:00 sharp in the morning.
   - You cannot be late.
   - You are allowed to bring 1 or 2 members of your family to look after you.

   - Be certain to have this ticket with you, otherwise you will not be admitted.

9. - The family decides Grandpa Joe should go with Charlie.

   Students need 2 of these answers.
   - He knows more about the factory than anyone else.
   - He deserves to go if he feels well enough.
   - Mrs. Bucket needed to stay at home with the other 3 old people.

Chapters 13 and 14

Page 27 A

Word	Part of Speech
1. fiend	noun
2. enraptured	adjective
3. dawdle	verb
4. velvet	noun
5. glimpse	noun
6. goatee	noun
7. climate	noun
8. corridor	noun
9. enchanted	adjective
10. charmed	adjective

Page 28 B

1. glimpse
2. enraptured
3. corridor
4. charmed
5. goatee
6. fiend
7. velvet
8. climate
9. dawdle

Pages 28-30 C
Sentences will vary.
   1. (in any order)

- All the other children, except Charlie, had their parents (mother and father) with them; Charlie had only Grandpa Joe.
- Charlie was waiting quietly while the other children had to be held back from trying to climb over the gates.

2. Violet Beauregarde – "She's still chewing that dreadful old piece of gum she's had for three months. Look at her jaws! They're still working on it."

   Augustus Gloop – "big fat boy," "Enormous, isn't he!"

   Mike Teavee – "picture of the Lone Ranger stenciled on his windbreaker." "He's the television fiend! He must be crazy! Look at all those crazy pistols he's got hanging all over him!"

   Veruca Salt – Her father "gives her anything she wants!" "She only has to start screaming for it and she gets it!" "The little girl in the silver mink coat!"

   Charlie Bucket – "He must be that skinny little shrimp." "Why hasn't he got a coat on in this cold weather?" "Maybe he can't afford to buy one." "He must be freezing!"

3. Students need 5 of these answers.
   - He had a black top hat on his head.
   - He wore a tailcoat made of a beautiful plum-colored velvet.
   - His trousers were bottle green.
   - His gloves were pearly gray.
   - In one hand, he carried a fine gold-topped walking cane.
   - He had a small neat pointed black beard—a goatee.
   - His eyes were marvelously bright; they seemed to be sparkling and twinkling.
   - His whole face was alight with fun and laughter.

4. He welcomed them to the factory. He asked to see each winner's ticket and greeted each one individually.

5. Answers may vary.
   a. Please don't wander off by yourself.
   b. He doesn't want to lose anyone at this stage of the proceedings.

6. The workers are used to an extremely hot climate—they'd perish in cold weather.

7.
   - 9 grown-ups (10 with Willy Wonka) and 5 children are in the group.
   - 14 people in all (15 with Willy Wonka).
   - They hustled and bustled down the passage trying to keep up with the swift Mr. Wonka.

8. a. Because they are headed underground—the most important rooms in the factory are deep down below the surface.
   b. (in any order)
   - They are enormous.
   - They are larger than football fields.
   - No building would be big enough to house them.

Chapters 15 and 16

Page 31 A

Across	Down
2. smuggled	1. flabbergasted
7. mischievous	3. peals
9. gorge	4. alders
10. eucalyptus	5. delectable
11. valley	6. froth
12. infested	8. insist

Page 32 B

1. verb	7. noun

2. noun
3. noun
4. noun
5. adjective
6. adjective

8. verb
9. noun
10. verb
11. verb
12. adjective

Pages 32-33 C

1. delectable
2. alders
5. froth
6. mischievous
7. peals
8. gorge

3. eucalyptus
4. insist
9. valley
10. smuggled
11. infested
12. flabbergasted

Pages 33-35 D
Sentences will vary.

1. Students need 4 answers; some possible answers are listed below.
   - They saw a lovely valley with green meadows on either side of the valley.
   - There was a flowing brown river with a tremendous waterfall halfway along.
   - Below the waterfall, there was a whole mass of enormous glass pipes.
   - There were graceful trees and bushes growing along the river banks.

2. His is the only factory that mixes its chocolate by waterfall.

3. Students need 8 of these answers.
   - astonishing sight
   - enormous glass pipes
   - brownish muddy water
   - never-ending suck-suck-sucking sound
   - graceful trees
   - weeping willows
   - tall clumps
   - pink, red, mauve blossoms
   - thousands of buttercups
   - gold-topped cane
   - great brown river
   - hot melted chocolate
   - finest quality (chocolate)
   - terrific (it)
   - entire country
   - swimming pools

4. She saw a little man walking down below the waterfall.

5. Students need 3 of these answers.
   - They were no higher than a knee
   - They laugh often.
   - They had funny long hair.
   - They were staring back at the visitors.
   - They were no larger than medium-sized dolls.

6. a. They were imported direct from Loompaland.
   b. There were thick jungles infested by the most dangerous beasts in the world (horswogglers, snozzwangers, and wicked whangdoodles). There were tree houses to escape from all of the beasts.

7. a. They liked to eat cacao beans.
   b. There was only a small supply of beans, so they had to eat the caterpillars.

8. Students need 2 of these answers.
   - He told them they could have all the cacao beans they wanted.
   - He would pay their wages in cacao beans if they wished.
   - They could have chocolate as well.

9.
   - They love dancing and music.
   - They make up songs.
   - They are mischievous.
   - They like jokes.
   - They all speak English.

10.
   - Veruca Salt screamed that she wanted an Oompa-Loompa. Her father agreed to get one for her.

- Augustus Gloop was on the riverbank drinking hot chocolate. His mother shouted that he'd better not be doing that.

Chapters 17 and 18

Page 36 A

Word	Part of Speech
1. infantile	adjective
2. inconceivable	adjective
3. liable	adjective
4. torpedo	noun
5. aghast	adjective
6. unutterably	adverb
7. indignantly	adverb
8. waggling	verb
9. brigade	noun
10. loathed	verb
11. Viking	noun
12. cogs	noun
13. vile	adjective

Page 37 B

1. brigade
2. unutterably
3. vile
4. infantile
5. indignantly
6. aghast
7. loathed
8. inconceivable
9. waggling
10. liable
11. Viking
12. cogs
13. torpedo

Pages 38-41 C
Sentences will vary.
1. • **Effect:** He fell in the river.
   • **Cause:** Augustus was very fat and enormous.
   Effect: He became stuck in the glass tube.
   • **Cause:** The pressure in the tube kept building up under Augustus.
   Effect: He was finally pushed up the tube.
2. • Mr. Wonka seemed cool, cold, and unfeeling towards the boy's situation. He didn't seem to take Mrs. Gloop's fears seriously and even joked about if the boy was made into fudge, it would taste terrible and no one would buy it. He didn't do anything to stop Augustus from being sucked up.
   • The Gloops, especially Mrs. Gloop, kept screaming at Mr. Wonka to do something. She was very upset that Mr. Wonka didn't seem to care about what happened to Augustus. She become more angry when Mr. Wonka just laughed.
3. a. Eating so much all the time is a bad thing.
   b. They planned on doing something to change Augustus.
4. Students need 3 of these answers.
   • It was pink.
   • It had a tall front and a tall back (like a Viking boat).
   • It was a row boat.
   • The ship had many oars on either side.
   • At least 10 Oompa-Loompas pulled each oar.
   • It sparkled, so it looked like it was made of glass.
5. a. Students need 5 of these answers.
   • The great chocolate river and the waterfall.
   • He saw Oompa-Loompas.
   • A beautiful pink boat.
   • The huge sucking pipes.

- Mr. Wonka himself.
- He saw candy meadows.

b. Charlie had never seen such peculiar and interesting people, places, and things before, and he wondered what else they could see that could possibly be more astonishing.

6. a. Mr. Wonka thinks they haven't been eating much.

b. As the hot chocolate ran down his throat, he felt very happy.

c. (in any order)
- He tells Charlie that he looks starved to death.
- He tells Grandpa Joe that he looks like a skeleton.
- He asks them both if they haven't had anything to eat in their house lately.

7. Answers will vary.
- When he sang that there's no "way of knowing which direction they are going," and that the Oompa-Loompas aren't slowing their rowing, it would have frightened me.
- The word "danger" would make me feel afraid that we could be hurt.

8. a. Use of words that are alike or nearly alike in sound but different in meaning.

b. (in any order)
- Storeroom Number 54—"hair cream"
- Storeroom Number 71—"whips..."
- Storeroom Number 77—"has beans" are the plays on words.

Chapters 19 and 20

Page 42 A

Word	Part of Speech
1. toffees	noun
2. suspended	verb

Word	Part of Speech
3. treacle	noun
4. meddling	verb
5. sensational	adjective
6. scrambled	verb
7. simmering	verb

Page 43 B

1. trading
2. coffees
3. cereal
4. flung
5. dimensional
6. walked
7. thinking

Pages 43-44 C

Sentences may vary.

1. a. The Inventing Room is the most important room.
- All of his secret new inventions are cooking and simmering in there.

b. He did not want any spies to steal his inventions/ideas.

2. Students need 3 of these answers.
- Kettles were hissing.
- Black metal pots were boiling and bubbling on huge stoves.
- Pans were sizzling.
- Strange iron machines were clanking and sputtering.
- Pipes were running all over the ceilings and walls.
- The whole place was filled with smoke and steam and delicious rich smells.

3. Yes, he loved this room most of all.

Students need 3 of these answers.
- He hopped around like a child among his Christmas presents.
- He lifted lids and sniffed what was cooking in them.

- He rushed to taste something in a barrel.
- He skipped to a machine and turned knobs.
- He peered into an oven, "rubbing his hands and cackling with delight."
- Then he ran over to a machine that was "phut-phutting" out little marble-sized balls.

4. • He invented Everlasting Gobstoppers.
   • He invented them for children with very little pocket money.

5. a. A huge beard started shooting out of his chin, and the beard grew so fast that soon it was trailing all over the floor in a thick hairy carpet.

   b. The mixture wasn't quite right.

   c. Some possible answers.
   • He is reckless.
   • He takes chances.
   • He is crazy.
   • He doesn't give up.

6. Students need 3 of these answers.
   • It was a mountain of gleaming metal.
   • Out of the very top sprouted hundreds and hundreds of thin glass tubes.
   • It towered high above the children and their parents.
   • The glass tubes came together in a bunch and hung suspended over an enormous round tub as big as a bath.

7. a. Students need 1 of these answers.
   • It was so small and thin and grey.
   • It looked like a strip of grey cardboard.
   • It was a stick of gum.

   b. Answers may vary; 1 possible answer is listed.
   • Everyone thought it might be a

mistake because the object was so small to be coming out of such a gigantic machine.

Chapters 21 and 22

Page 45 A

Word	Part of Speech
1. repulsive	adjective
2. spellbound	adjective
3. wafting	verb
4. ludicrous	adjective
5. sanatorium	noun
6. obstinately	adverb
7. gaping	verb

Page 46 B

1. spellbound
2. wafting
3. ludicrous
4. obstinately
5. repulsive
6. sanatorium
7. gaping

Pages 46-48 C

Sentences will vary.

1. a. His latest invention is a tiny piece of gum that is a three-course dinner all by itself.

   b. Students need 3 of these answers.
   • It would mean the end of all kitchens and cooking.
   • No plates would be needed.
   • There would be no more marketing to do.
   • No washing up.
   • No more buying of meat and groceries.
   • No garbage to take out.
   • No knives and forks at mealtime.
   • No mess to clean up.

2. Students need 4 of these answers.
   Mr. Wonka:
   - He told her not to take it because it wasn't ready yet.
   - He said to spit it out.
   - He began wringing his hands and begged her to stop chewing it.

   Parents:
   - Mrs. Beauregarde thought it was an interesting experience.
   - She told Violet that she's a clever girl.
   - Mr. Beauregarde told her to keep chewing.
   - He was proud that she was the first person to try the gum.

3. • Violet first tasted soup, then roast beef, then buttery potato.
   - Her last taste was of blueberry pie and cream
   - She felt like she'd actually swallowed the food.
   - Her nose and then her cheeks turned blue then purple.
   - She turned purple/violet all over.
   - She started to swell up and felt sick.
   - Her body swelled up into an enormous, round ball.
   - All that remained of Violet the girl were her legs, arms, and head sticking out of the ball.

4. a. He wanted them to take her to the Juicing Room.
   b. They'd squeeze all of the juice out of her.

5. a. Her massive jaws bit her tongue in two.
   b. (in any order)
   - They don't want Violet to end up like Miss Bigelow.
   - They think she's still young enough to change.

6. Mike Teavee and Veruca Salt are the two remaining "naughty" children.

Mike's bad behaviors are watching TV all the time and wanting to be a hooligan. Veruca wants her parents to give her anything she wants, and she wants everything she sees.
(The paragraphs that students write need to involve "accidents" that directly relate to these bad habits.)

7. (in any order)
   - Eatable Marshmallow Pillows are soft pillows that you can eat.
   - Lickable Wallpaper for Nurseries is wallpaper you can lick and taste whatever is pictured on it.
   - Hot Ice Creams for Cold Days warms you up in freezing weather.
   - Cows That Give Chocolate Milk are pretty little cows that produce chocolate milk.
   - Fizzy Lifting Drinks are drinks filled with special gas bubbles that lift you off the ground.

Chapters 23 and 24

Page 49 A

Word	Part of Speech
1. triumphantly	adjective
2. tiddly	adjective
3. frump	noun
4. pandered	verb
5. culprits	noun
6. incinerator	noun
7. halibut	noun
8. anchored	verb

Page 50 B

1. tipsy
2. spoiled
3. lawbreakers
4. successfully
5. furnace
6. dull woman

7. flatfish
8. fastened

Pages 50-52 C
Sentences will vary.
1. • The Salt family was the most argumentative.
   • Mrs. Salt accused Mr. Wonka of lying.
   • Mr. Wonka called her an old fish and told her to go boil her head.
   • Mrs. Salt was outraged and said, "How dare you speak to me like that!"
   • Mr. Wonka replied rudely, "Oh, do shut up!"
2. a. When Mr. Wonka entered the room, the faces of the square candies looked toward the door and stared at Mr. Wonka—they "look (a)round".
   b. The candies are actually shaped like a square (cube), not shaped round. The people thought Mr. Wonka was saying the candies were shaped both square and round at the same time which would be impossible—Mr. Wonka was using a play on words.
3. If they go in, they'll disturb the squirrels that are busy shelling walnuts.
4. Students need 3 of these answers
   • 100 squirrels were seated upon high stools around a large table.
   • Mounds and mounds of nuts were piled on the table.
   • The squirrels were all working away like mad.
   • The squirrels were shelling walnuts at a tremendous speed.
5. (in any order)
   • Oompa-Loompas can't get walnuts out of walnut shells in one piece.
   • They always break them in two.
   • Nobody except squirrels can get

walnuts whole out of walnut shells every time.
6. a. They tap each walnut with their knuckles.
   • Bad nuts make a hollow sound.
   b. They don't open a bad nut—they just throw it down the garbage chute.
7. a. She was spoiled.
   b. Anytime she wants something (a Golden Ticket, an Oompa-Loompa, or a trained squirrel), her parents say they'll get it for her.
8. Students need 3 of these answers.
   • Every squirrel jumped on her and pinned her down.
   • One squirrel tapped her head with its knuckles.
   • They started carrying her across the floor.
   • Mr. Wonka said Veruca "is a bad nut after all," and, "her head must have sounded quite hollow."
   • Every single squirrel around the table took a flying leap towards her and landed on her body
   • 25 caught her right arm and held it down.
   • 25 caught her left arm and pinned it down.
   • 25 caught her left leg and anchored it down.
   • 24 caught her right leg.
   • 1 climbed on her shoulder and started tap-tap-tapping her head with its knuckles.
9. They tested her to see if she was a bad nut.
10. (in any order)
    • Mr. Wonka expected that "someone will catch them at the bottom of the chute."
    • He said the Oompa-Loompas only light the fire every other day.
    • He said it was probably one of the days when the incinerator fire

isn't lit.

b. Neither of them wanted anyone to actually be killed.

11. Students need 1 of these answers.
   - They spoiled her.
   - They pandered to her every need.
   - They were responsible for turning her into a brat.

Chapters 25 and 26

Page 53 A

Word	Part of Speech
1. precipice	noun
2. gallantly	adverb
3. flickered	verb
4. tamper	verb
5. craggy	adjective
6. hurtled	verb
7. jujubes	noun

Pages 54 B

Explanations may vary, some possible answers are listed.

1. True, <u>jujubes</u> are candy and candy is sold in movie theaters.
2. False, <u>gallantly</u> means to behave politely and shoving a person is not polite.
3. False, since a <u>precipice</u> is a nearly vertical cliff, sledding would be extremely dangerous.
4. True, <u>hurtled</u> means to be thrown forcefully.
5. True, <u>craggy</u> means steep and rugged, which many mountains are.
6. False, if you <u>tampered</u> with something you change it without permission, and this would not please your neighbor.
7. False, it would be harder to read with lights that <u>flickered</u> or went off and on.

Pages 54-57 C

1. a. Mike Teavee, Charlie Bucket, Mr. Teavee, Mrs. Teavee, and Grandpa Joe remained with the tour.

   b. The children will be all right after they have been through their "clean-up."

2. Because Mike Teavee says his feet are getting tired and that he wants to watch television.

3. Students need 3 of these answers.
   - The walls and even the ceiling were covered all over with rows and rows of small, black push buttons (thousands).
   - Every single button had a tiny printed label beside it telling which room you would be taken to if you pressed it.
   - The elevator can go sideways and longways and slantways and any other way you can think of.
   - The whole elevator is made of thick, clear glass.

4. a. He pushed the Television Chocolate button.

   b. Students need 2 of these answers.
   - There was a tremendous whizzing noise.
   - The doors clanged shut.
   - The elevator leaped away as though it had been stung by a wasp.
   - It leapt sideways, flinging the passengers off their feet and onto the floor.

5. Students need 3 of these answers.
   - An enormous spout with brown sticky stuff oozing out of it onto the floor.
   - A great craggy mountain made entirely of fudge with Oompa-Loompas hacking huge hunks out of its side.

- A machine with white powder spraying out of it like a snowstorm.
- A lake of hot caramel with steam coming off it.
- A village of Oompaa-Loompas, with tiny houses and streets and hundreds of Oompa-Loompa children no more than 4 inches high playing in the streets.

6. They are worried about a collision, because Mr. Wonka tells them about another elevator that goes the opposite way on the same track.

7. A pair of dark glasses, because the light in the room could blind them.

8. Students need 5 of these answers.
   - It was a long narrow room.
   - The room was painted white all over.
   - There wasn't a speck of dust anywhere.
   - The room was completely bare except for the far ends.
   - Huge lamps hung down from the ceiling and bathed the room in a brilliant blue-white light.
   - There was an enormous camera on wheels with a whole army of Oompa-Loompas clustering around it.
   - A single Oompa-Loompa was sitting at a black table gazing at the screen of a very large television set.

9. a. They were wearing bright-red space suits, helmets, and goggles.
   b. (in any order)
   - They weren't chattering or singing like they usually did.
   - They moved slowly and carefully.
   - They worked in complete silence.

10. - He wanted to send a real bar of chocolate whizzing through the air in tiny pieces and then put the pieces together at the other end,

ready to be eaten.
- He saw a television working and thought people can break up a photograph into millions of pieces, send the pieces whizzing though the air, and put them together at the other end.

11. Because whenever something is sent by television, it always comes out much smaller than it was when it went in.

12. a. The suits protect them.
    b. They could be broken up into a million tiny pieces in one second.

13. - He reached out, touched the television screen, and miraculously pulled the bar of chocolate away in his fingers.

Chapters 27 and 28

Page 58 A

Across	Down
2. craned	1. arrangements
3. nauseating	4. loll
5. elastic	
6. splintering	

Page 59 B

Word	Part of Speech
1. craned	verb
2. arrangements	noun
3. loll	verb
4. nauseating	adjective
5. splintering	adjective
6. elastic	adjective

Pages 59-63 C
Sentences will vary.

1. a. Of course it could, but it might have some very nasty results.
   b. Mike ran towards the other end of the room where the camera

was standing, shouting that he would be the first person in the world to be sent by television.

2. Students need 5 of these answers.
   - He jumped straight for the switch.
   - He scattered Oompa-Loompas right and left.
   - He shouted, "See you later, alligator!"
   - He pulled down the switch.
   - He leaped out into the full glare of the lens.
   - He disappeared.

3. He told them that sometimes only about half the small pieces find their way into the television set.

4. Students need 2 of these answers.
   - Mrs. Teavee thinks only half of Mike is coming back.
   - Mrs. Teavee screamed in horror.
   - Mr. Teavee hoped the top half of his son would come back.

5. (in any order)
   - He's shrunk like a midget.
   - He has a tiny voice like a squeaking mouse.

6. (in any order)
   - Mrs. Teavee says Mike won't be able to do anything (with his small size).
   - Mr. Teavee says that he's throwing the television set right out the window the moment they get home.

7. a. He wants to put Mike in a special machine that he has for testing the stretchiness of chewing gum.
   b. Because small boys are extremely springy and elastic.

8. Students need 5 of these answers.
   - It rots the senses in the head.
   - It kills imagination dead.
   - It clogs and clutters up the mind.
   - It makes a child so dull and blind, he can no longer understand a

fantasy or fairyland.
   - A child's brain becomes as soft as cheese.
   - A child's powers of thinking rust and freeze.
   - A child cannot think, he only sees.

9. a. Throw them away.
   b. A lovely bookshelf on the wall.
   c. Yes or no and explanation.

10. - Only Charlie is left.
    - He wins.

11. a. Jump in the great glass elevator.
    b. He was really excited because he thought something crazy was going to happen.

12. Students need 3 of these answers
    - The glass doors closed.
    - The elevator shot straight up like a rocket.
    - They traveled straight up with no twistings or turnings.
    - Charlie could hear the whistling of air as the elevator went faster and faster.

13. - If it doesn't travel any faster, they will never break through the roof of the factory.

14. (in any order)
    - The elevator rose into the sky like a rocket.
    - Sunshine was pouring in through the glass roof.
    - In 5 seconds, they were a thousand feet in the sky.

15. Students need 2 of these answers
    - The elevator stopped.
    - It hung in the air.
    - It was hovering like a helicopter.

Chapters 29 and 30

Page 64 A

Word	Part of Speech
1. despair	verb
2. hovering	verb
3. petrified	adjective
4. cocked	verb
5. brim	noun

Page 65 B

1. despair
2. petrified
3. hovering
4. brim
5. cocked

Page 65-67 C

Sentences will vary.

1. • They were going to take each Golden Ticket winner and his or her parents home.
   • They were filled with the first delivery of the child's lifetime supply of candy.

2. (in any order)
   • Augustus Gloop is now as thin as a straw because he was squeezed through the chocolate sucking tube.
   • Violet Beauregarde is purple in the face from chewing the blueberry pie gum.
   • Veruca Salt is covered with garbage from being tossed down the garbage chute.
   • Mike Teavee is ten feet tall and as thin as a wire from the stretching machine.

3. Because every basketball team in the country will want Mike because he is now so tall.

4. • He thinks it is the most wonderful place in the world.

   • As soon as Charlie is old enough to run it, the entire factory will be his.

5. Students need 2 of these answers.
   • Mr. Wonka is an old man.
   • He can't go on forever.
   • Mr. Wonka has no children or family of his own.
   • Someone has to keep the factory going, if only for the sake of the Oompa-Loompas.

6. Students need 3 of these answers
   • A grown-up won't listen to him.
   • A grown-up won't learn.
   • A grown-up will try to do things his way and not Mr. Wonka's.
   • He wants a good sensible loving child to whom he can tell all of his most precious candy-making secrets while he is still alive.

7. He decided to invite 5 children to the factory and the one he liked best at the end of the day would be the winner (and get the factory).

8. a. Charlie is afraid his mother won't come with them to the factory because she won't leave Grandma Josephine, Grandma Georgina, and Grandpa George.
   b. He wants to take the bed the grandparents are in, along with them, in the elevator.

9. By crashing the elevator through the roof and taking the bed in the elevator.

10. (in any order)
   • Mr. Wonka, Grandpa Joe, and Charlie all pushed the bed into the elevator.
   • They pushed Mr. and Mrs. Bucket in after it.

11. Answers may vary; 1 possible answer is listed.
   • Nearly everything there is edible.

Extension Activity 1

Answers will vary.

Extension Activity 2

1. The story is told with an abundance of fantasy but is held within the outline of a sense of realism. There is a huge contrast between the real life of Charlie—even the lives of the spoiled children—and the life Willie Wonka lives within the factory.

   In addition, the words—real and made-up—used by Roald Dahl throughout the book make it even more fantastic. The entire concept of the Chocolate Factory is based on bright colors, oddities, tastes, and sounds, all of which pull us farther and farther away from the real life lived by Charlie.

   The ultimate enjoyment of this story is probably the wonderfulness of a poor, underprivileged family being given a new life of riches and wonder.

2. No, Charlie has no bad habits. The children in the book are either good or bad. Charlie is good. Augustus is greedy, Veruca is bratty, Violet is an obsessive gum chewer, and Mike is obsessed with television.

   Charlie speaks only when he is spoken to. He never asks for more than he is given. He is respectful of his parents and grandparents. He takes time to enjoy his once-a-year candy bar bite by bite, instead of wolfing it down all at once. When he's starving, he doesn't complain but finds ways to deal with it.

3. He doesn't criticize the way the children came by their Golden Tickets, except to comment on Veruca's father's method as being "not quite fair." Charlie handles his poverty with diginity and his good luck with a sense of fascination rather than believing it is owed to him.

   Charlie faces the mysteries of the factory with the same bravery he employs to overcome the adversity of his everyday life. He finds the chocolate factory to be wonderful but doesn't take advantage of the things it offers.

4. He believes it is not a bad child's fault that he is bad—his parents are mostly to blame. So, the parents should suffer as well as the children. In this story, the proper punishment is the only thing that can transform a bad child into a good one.

5. They are very close in the beginning of the story and very dependent on each other for love and support. In the last part of the story, Grandpa Joe begins to be less approving of Mr. Wonka's ways, while Charlie becomes more involved. Grandpa Joe admired Mr. Wonka's role as a mentor for Charlie. Mr. Wonka draws Charlie away from the dependence he had on his Grandfather. Mr. Wonka essentially takes Grandpa Joe's place.

6. He's made up of opposites. He is old but full of energy and a sense of fun. He is physically small, but his personality is larger than life. He is both charming and insensitive, as the reader can tell by the way he talks to and treats his guests individually. He can be extremely demanding and judgmental. The four children who

do not win the grand prize clearly disgust Mr. Wonka.

Mr. Wonka's good side shows in the way he rescued the Oompa-Loompas and gave them such a good life in his factory. He seems to like children better than adults and shows this by choosing a child to take over his factory.

7. It could be compared to slavery in that Mr. Wonka took the Oompa-Loompas from their homeland to serve him in his factory. However, since they were being threatened, eaten, and starved, he did save them. They are given everything they need and seem to enjoy their new life. However, he doesn't let them out of the factory, and that seems more like a type of slavery than protection.

8. Children should not be given everything they want. They should be respectful of adults. They shouldn't focus only on one thing, like chewing gum or television.

9. Poverty versus wealth plays a part in the moral of the story. Even if you're poor and small, you can be a better person than those who are rich. The chocolate factory shows great wealth, while Charlie's home life shows great poverty. The wealthy turn out to be bad people, but the poor person, Charlie, is good and rewarded for that quality in the end.
If you're good, good things will come to you.

10. It would depend upon the adult. Dahl's writing style is like comedy. The whole idea is odd, but it's easy to become caught up in Dahl's imagination. Adults might be more likely to enjoy the book more than the movie from the writing point of view. The movie is more like a cartoon, and much of the literary style is overwhelmed by the visuals.